painted furniture

Decorating Ideas & Projects

Better Homes and Gardens® Books
Des Moines, Iowa

Better Homes and Gardens® Books
An imprint of Meredith® Books

Painted Furniture
Editor: Linda Hallam
Design: The Design Office of Jerry J. Rank
Contributing Editors: Susan Andrews, Andrea Caughey, Joetta Moulden
Project Designers: Tina Blanck, Brian Carter, Deborah Hastings, Patricia Mohr Kramer, Amy
 Queen, Wade Scherrer, Donna Talley Wendt
Copy Chief: Terri Fredrickson
Book Production Managers: Pam Kvitne, Marjorie J. Schenkelberg
Contributing Copy Editor: Lorraine Ferrell
Contributing Proofreaders: Jean Ellis, Garland Walton, Willa Speiser
Contributing Photographers: Fran Brennan, Randy Foulds, Tria Giovan, Ed Gohlich,
 Bob Greenspan, Pete Krumhardt, Emily Minton
Indexer: Kathleen Poole
Electronic Production Coordinator: Paula Forest
Editorial and Design Assistants: Kaye Chabot, Mary Lee Gavin, Karen Schirm

Meredith® Books
Editor in Chief: James D. Blume
Design Director: Matt Strelecki
Managing Editor: Gregory H. Kayko
Executive Shelter Editor: Denise L. Caringer

Director, Retail Sales and Marketing: Terry Unsworth
Director, Sales, Special Markets: Rita McMullen
Director, Sales, Premiums: Michael A. Peterson
Director, Sales, Retail: Tom Wierzbicki
Director, Book Marketing: Brad Elmitt
Director, Operations: George A. Susral
Director, Production: Douglas M. Johnston

Vice President, General Manager: Jamie L. Martin

Better Homes and Gardens® **Magazine**
Editor in Chief: Jean LemMon
Executive Interior Design Editor: Sandra S. Soria

Meredith Publishing Group
President, Publishing Group: Stephen M. Lacy
Vice President, Finance and Administration: Max Runciman

Meredith Corporation
Chairman and Chief Executive Officer: William T. Kerr

Chairman of the Executive Committee: E. T. Meredith III

Cover Photograph: Pete Krumhardt

All of us at Better Homes and Gardens® Books are dedicated to providing you with information
and ideas to enhance your home. We welcome your comments and suggestions. Write to us at:
Better Homes and Gardens Books, Shelter Editorial Department, 1716 Locust St., Des Moines,
IA 50309-3023.

If you would like to purchase any of our books, check wherever quality books are sold. Visit us
online at bhg.com.

contents

getting started

Smart decorators are turning to painted furniture to transform their rooms. Painted furniture is not only **stylish and fun, but also affordable.** With a few cans of paint and a little practice, you can give a slightly tired furniture piece new life. And budget-friendly, unfinished furniture can grace the most fashionable settings.

To help you get started, look through this book to **see how**  **painted furniture enlivens every room of the house**—from the entry through the living areas and bedrooms to the porch and patio. You'll see that painted furniture **looks lively and current** in a variety of settings—from traditional to country cottage—in new and vintage houses. **Painted furniture mixes** well with stained wood and upholstered furnishings too.

To experience the decorating potential of painted furniture, turn to the medley of settings and ideas for living and dining areas, bedrooms and baths, including children's rooms and nurseries, and outdoor spaces in Chapters One through Four. **Painted furniture is especially appealing in bedrooms,** the most personal of spaces. A romantic white-on-white theme is both sophisticated and easy to create with varying shades of white paint. **Cottage-style bedrooms** appear fresh and youthful when you give softly colored painted pieces starring roles. Nurseries and children's bedrooms lend themselves **to the charm and fancy** that are created easily with painted furniture. From the cheerful room featured here and on pages 4–5 (project directions on page 78) to the profusion of rooms in varying themes and color palette ranges, you'll find **illustrative ideas and fashionable motifs.**

Create an entire room of painted furniture or just add small accents, such as lamp tables in the living room or a chest of drawers in a bedroom. With so many **clever color choices to consider,** you can refresh a rocking chair or Adirondack chair to luxuriate in on your porch or deck. Although classic Scandinavian and American country furniture are especially compatible with painted furniture, you'll discover many styles lend themselves to painted finishes.

Chapter Five presents complete directions for the featured projects, accompanied by skill and time estimates, supply lists, and sources. **Expert tips from project designers** will help you achieve professional results. After choosing your favorite color palette, you'll learn simple techniques that will **transform plain furniture pieces into personal treasures to use in your home.** As you **update and energize your furniture** with paint and details, you'll discover this decorator secret: **Every paintable piece has potential.**

living&dining

Turn to paint to transform flea market finds
and unfinished buys into fashion furnishings.

◆living&dining

FUN IN CALIFORNIA. Create the living room that fits
your taste and lifestyle by mixing painted furnishings to
showcase inexpensive finds. Look for furniture that is
compatible in scale and spirit no matter what its style or
era. For the easiest start, anchor your scheme with one or
two focal pieces and work from there. Forget the maxim
of small furniture in a small room. Pick a few larger tables
or chairs. Feel free to mix new and old pieces with your
own painted furniture creations. For interesting pieces
that have discreetly peeling paint, brush away loose paint
to avoid paint chips. If you have children in your home,
seal such furniture with a matte polyurethane to avoid
contact with old lead-based paint. (All new paints are
lead-free.) Paint walls a vibrant color and add favorite
collectibles from flea markets to design a welcoming
living room and dining area.

◆ An overscaled architectural-salvage coffee table
balances the painted metal daybed in this cottage living
room and shows off its fashionably aged finish through
the transparent glass on the tabletop. White paint
freshens the flea market curved sewing cabinet and
the crisp woodwork, providing contrast for the buttercup
yellow and rich red painted walls.

◆ Floral fabrics in the slipcovered armchair, cushions,
pillows, and balloon shades soften the room and add
cottage appeal. The romantic setting is emphasized and
personalized with a patterned rug, canine collectibles,
and a vintage dollhouse.

FUN IN CALIFORNIA. Look for painted pieces to fit your spaces. If you can't find the right piece, broaden your search to include unfinished or secondhand furniture to paint and detail to your own specifications. Accent pieces by local artists are an interesting way to introduce painted furniture into your home.

◆ Found at a California flea market, a green armoire with peeling paint, *right,* fits a shallow wall in a small cottage. The trio of miniature Adirondack chairs serves as a reminder of summer fun. **See page 85 for artistic armoire project.**

◆ Stenciled cornflower blue flowers adorn a vintage painted sewing cabinet, *below.* Bright daisies provide an element of surprise and the inspiration for the fresh flower arrangement on this versatile piece of furniture.

◆ Yellow and red walls, *left and below,* create an upbeat background for the metal table taped and painted by a local artist. Such bold color pairings energize rooms filled with white furniture or other neutral pieces. **See page 89 for a painted metal table project.**

◆ The harlequin-patterned accent table, *above and below,* pairs a scrolled, bistro-style base with a taped-off and painted top. Coats of clear polyurethane ensure long wear and protect against scratches. The Eiffel Tower model, from a Paris flea market, dresses up the arrangement.

◆ New furniture crafted from salvaged components elevates vintage furniture to new heights. The coffee table, *above,* shows off intricate detailing of the Victorian era. Peeling paint—overlaid with glass on the top—adds to the charm.

FUN IN CALIFORNIA. Freshen living or dining areas by painting a built-in to serve as the contrast to painted furniture pieces. Use crisp white to lighten and brighten small rooms or rooms with little natural light. Choose a pretty wall color that works with the colors of your painted pieces. When you can't narrow your color choices to one or two, embrace diversity by painting dining chairs in a medley of your favorite lively shades. Paint one chair style in three or four compatible colors, or choose chairs that combine styles and detailing.

◆ Three different tinted stains transform inexpensive chairs, *opposite,* into an upbeat personal design statement. The opaque stains enrich with color while allowing subtle hints of wood grains to show through. A rugged farm table with a protective glass top is an appropriate companion to the rainbow hues of chairs. **See page 79 for techniques.**

◆ Shapely chairs, purchased unfinished, recall the country styles of 19th-century France, Italy, and Sweden—and contribute a stylish touch to the dining room. The built-in cabinet, *right,* has been updated with white paint, after sanding and priming, to cover the original dark, heavy stain. It makes its new appearance as a handy storage piece and room divider in a comfortable family cottage.

◆ Vibrant color turns a basic, unpainted dining chair, *below right,* into a striking design statement. Raw wood soaks up yellow stain for deep color; a second coat and matte varnish guarantee long wear and durability.

SWEDISH STYLE. Mix new reproduction painted furniture with vintage pieces that you update with paint and detailing. Stretch your decorating dollars and your creativity by painting pieces you already own rather than purchasing all new pieces. For inspiration, choose a style that appeals to you—such as a light and spare Swedish style—and forget concerns about strict historical interpretations. Strive to create a pleasant mood and inviting, friendly rooms to live in and enjoy.

◆ Old and new mix harmoniously in this classic blue and white, Swedish-inspired dining room, *opposite.* Reproduction Queen Anne-style chairs, originally stained dark, are freshened with creamy white paint. The 20th-century reproduction sideboard has been cleaned and painted for fresh use. New reproduction pieces—the plate rack and dining table—exhibit an aged finish as well as classic straight legs and beaded trim, derived from Swedish antiques.

See page 111 for sources.

◆ In decorating and home furnishings, blue and white are set off with sunny yellow, *below left.*

◆ A Swedish-motif stencil, *below right,* works as well on classic chairs as on furniture made by 18th- and 19th-century European furnituremakers.

◆ The delicate mirror sconces that reflect candlelight, *right,* illustrate the innovative and beautiful ways Swedish craftspeople illuminated long winter nights and gray days.

TRANSFERWARE-INSPIRED. Enjoy your collections even more by combining them with painted furniture pieces based on your treasure hunts. Whether your passion is for pottery, porcelain, or textiles, mirror the motifs and colors in inspired creations detailed with handpainted motifs. If you prefer not to hand-paint, echo the colors of your favorite collectibles in the shades and simple painting techniques that you choose for your furniture. Detail the furniture with contrasting colors, and use stenciled or stamped motifs appropriate to your collection.

◆ A clever collector has duplicated stylized motifs of brown and cream to embellish a painted, distressed, and color-washed unfinished armoire, *right.* **See page 79 for techniques.**

◆ Cabinet doors, *below,* are framed with paint to match the molding trim and to emphasize the pottery patterns. Decorative pulls complement the drag technique used on the drawers.

◆ An easily accomplished distressed technique unifies an oak table—a flea market bargain because of its damaged top—and four European country-style unfinished chairs, *above*. Primer is allowed to soak into the unfinished wood, causing a slightly pickled effect that allows some grain to show. The paint and chairs transform a country table into a sophisticated grouping. **See page 80 for techniques; see page 112 for chair source.**

◆ The sturdy curves of the chair, *left*, typical of 19th century European country furniture, are compatible with the American oak table. The proliferation of well-made unfinished furniture makes it easy to mix new and vintage pieces with the artistry of paint.

BURLED AND AGED. Warm and relax a traditional room with a painted table as a significant accent piece. Choose rich colors to work with a rug or other furnishings as well as the wall color and other major furniture pieces. An interestingly shaped table, painted with shiny black or brown enamel, or finished to resemble 19th-century graining techniques, makes a strong decorating statement.

◆ Purchased unfinished, this sturdy coffee table, *above,* emulates the visual appeal of burled wood. The painted legs provide a contrast to the decorative top. The scale balances the upholstered pieces and adds visual weight to the grouping. **See page 83 for techniques.**

◆ The simplified version of the graining technique, accomplished with glaze and cheesecloth, echoes the elements of the traditional living room. A layer of polyurethane allows the generously scaled table, *opposite above,* to stand up to the rigors of everyday use.

◆ The antiqued finish updates this reproduction French provincial-style table, *bottom*. The details of the table apron and legs readily absorb glaze for an ornate look. Reproduction furniture made after World War II is easily found at tag and garage sales as well as secondhand shops and thrift stores. Choose furniture pieces that are in good condition, that require a minimum of repairs, and that are not sealed with plastic-type laminates. **See page 84 for techniques.**

SWEDISH LINEN. Refine cabinets with paint techniques that convert freestanding or built-in units into stylish furniture. For such pieces to serve as low-key backdrops for collections, paint them to match other woodwork in the room. To make them focal points within the room, give pieces subtle, yet interesting, paint finishes or embellish the trim.

◆ A new paint job for this desk, *right,* with built-in storage above transforms a once-dark corner into a chic home office and study nook. Departing from the standard, a finish painted to emulate linen fabric graces the unit. The chair keeps its original stained finish but is updated with plaid and floral fabric in complementary colors. **See page 82 for techniques.**

◆ Delicate hand-painted details and faceted glass pulls, *below,* provide the attention that turn standard painted furniture into memorable accent pieces.

◆ Crackling is a popular finish that "ages" new pieces, allowing the base to show through small irregular cracks, *below*. Crackling is an appropriate background finish for collectibles.

◆ An easily accomplished crackling technique adds the charm of antique furniture to an unfinished cupboard placed in a combination breakfast room and kitchen, *left*. The ivory-over oak scheme serves as the perfect contrast for a collection of 19th-century brown and cream transferware. Painting the base color to complement a collection further enhances that collection. A collector of blue and white transferware, for example, might choose a clear medium blue base coat. As alternatives, only the inside of the unit could be crackled, the inside could be painted a contrasting shade, or only the sides and drawers could be crackled. **See page 80 for techniques.**

VICTORIAN REVIVAL. If late 19th- or early 20th-century furniture seems too dark or heavy for your decor, bring it into the 21st century with fresh white paint. (Keep in mind that painting a valuable antique lowers its value. If you think a piece is an authentic antique, check with a reputable dealer before painting or altering its finish.) As you shop for bargain pieces to paint, look for furniture that has interesting trim or detailing that will highlight well with paint. Disregard dated fabrics on chair backs and seats. Contemporary fabrics, in lively 21st century colors, provide the final transformation. For the best results, always sand and prime stained or painted pieces. Choose a shade of white or cream that works with your wall colors, fabrics, and accessories.

◆ A creamy shade of white enamel lightens and brightens a previously dark-stained dresser and a pair of flea market dining chairs, *opposite*. Even the country-style shelf bracket is painted to coordinate with the lighthearted, cheerful setting.

◆ Designers are transforming dark Eastlake-style furniture into fashionable accent pieces with white paint and fabrics. The hall table and straight chair, classic Eastlake pieces, stand out against a sunny yellow background, *below*.

◆ Painted white and then antiqued, an inherited hall table and mirror, *top right*, provide ample background for a prized 19th-century dresser bowl and water pitcher.

◆ White paint updates early 20th century furniture, *below right*, for a cheerful setting that welcomes guests. Floral fabric contribute to the airy appeal.

ARTISTIC ARMOIRES. Conceal your television and other electronic equipment while creating a decorative focal point with a painted armoire or wardrobe. Such storage pieces are good buys as unfinished furniture. Unlike vintage finds, new armoires are often sized to hold contemporary electronic equipment. Always measure your television and other equipment, and measure new or vintage pieces to ensure adequate interior spaces. The crucial measurement is for depth because some cabinets aren't deep enough for standard televisions.

◆ A combination of taping and hand-painting results in energizing motifs for this stock unfinished armoire, *opposite*. You can either stencil or stamp similar motifs. Lively pieces work best in settings where they assume a starring role, as other furnishings become supporting players. Two cheerful primary colors enliven the setting—the bright red contrasting with the yellow-striped walls. **See page 84 for techniques.**

◆ To conceal the television, a subtle weathered finish allows the large armoire, *below,* to blend rather than stand out as a design element. Because the Oriental-style rug and the fabrics are the room's focal points, the painted armoire doesn't compete. **See page 85 for techniques.**

FRENCH BLUE AND WHITE. Enrich your dining room by painting one or two key pieces to impart French charm. In this era of personal decorating, consider painting an interesting piece you own, or shop for vintage or unfinished pieces that would work in the style and scale of your existing furnishings. As a starting point, look to elements that you already own, such as wallpaper, rugs, or a collection. Choose pieces that complement rather than match existing pieces in the room. Finding your personal style will be fun and rewarding.

◆ Originally too dark for a French-style room, detailed blue sideboard, *above and right,* now adds buoyancy to the traditional-style dining room. Wallpaper, porcelains, and the rug inspired the colors. Deep drawers and sturdy construction make it ideal for linen and flatware storage. **See page 86 for techniques.**

◆ A collection of blue and white pottery and porcelain determines the color scheme for a cozy breakfast area *below,* where sturdy, unfinished chairs are painted four shades of blue enamel. The table, an unfinished piece chosen for its gently curving legs and apron, sports a sponged top and a simple edging detail. The four shades of blue aptly illustrate that you can create a one-of-a-kind look with paint and basic techniques. For an extra decorative accent, a stenciled fleur-de-lis motif graces the back of each chair; a stylized flower or a motif selected from the blue and white pottery would work equally well. Floral and striped fabrics adorn seat cushions and pillows. **See pages 81–82 for techniques.**

RUSTIC RETREAT. Rummaging through your attic, a secondhand store, or an antiques shop may uncover the perfect paintable furniture to accent your informal living and dining spaces. You may need only to clean pieces that will become welcome additions into your home. Brush dirty pieces lightly, then scrub gently with mild soap and water. If young children will use or play around the pieces, prevent contact with lead paint by brushing off all loose or chipping paint. Use polyurethane to seal the furniture. **See page 111 for sources.**

◆ A worktable with a drawer, *above left*, adds storage and charm while doubling as a lamp table. Space under the leggy

table is put to use to store functional and decorative boxes.

◆ A painted accent chair, *opposite, above right,* adds stylish charm to the decor. Small, practical pieces can be used in many settings—porches, bedrooms, entry halls, and dining areas. Accent chairs of differing styles can be painted in similar colors to mix and match, creating a coordinated look within the room. Use decorative chairs in place of small tables to hold books, frames, plants, and other aesthetic items.

◆ Painted chairs relax a dining room while comfortably pairing with a natural wood table, *opposite, below.* The contrasting blue sideboard is indicative of the color and charm of the American country and colonial styles of painted furniture. Accessories such as metalware and quilts, shown in cool shades of blue and green, create a restful palette, allowing cow paintings to become a design statement. Barn red and buttery yellow are also typical country colors.

◆ Assembled from porch columns and architectural trim, the pale green country-style étagère, *above,* furnishes whimsy on a large scale within a living and dining area full of eclectic furnishings and collectibles. The soft green echoes the floral print fabric covering the mid-20th-century upholstered armchair. This one-of-a-kind painted piece, definitely a find for a collector who needs display space, neatly organizes an array of boxes and painted tole accessories **See page 111 for shop sources.**

PALE SOPHISTICATES. Search for paintable furniture that has decorating potential at flea markets, secondhand stores, and antiques shops. Select pieces that are in scale, proportion, and are of appropriate style for the room and furnishings into which you plan to incorporate them. Examine pieces for sturdiness and reasonably good condition, allowing for minor repairs. For furniture that you plan to paint, determine whether the surfaces are paintable, whether obvious damage can be repaired, and whether the repairs merit the cost and the work involved. For previously painted furniture, you may only need to sand rough spots and prime before repainting in your color choice. **See page 89 for previously painted furniture projects.**

◆ A promising find from a vintage furniture store, the Swedish-style day bed, *opposite,* is updated with a cushion, bolster, and pillows to enhance a living room. Such worthwhile investments fit into a variety of settings.

◆ Bold stripes created with painter's tape and two shades of paint transform a vintage 1920s-era chest into a handsome traditional room accent, *above.* Gold- and silver-tone paint defines the chest and emphasizes the delicately turned legs on this period piece.

◆ Aging and distressing techniques produce a cupboard that reflects a refined rustic setting, *above right.* Reproduction pulls furnish an authentic touch, and color-washed walls provide a contrast for the distinctive furniture.
See page 88 for a similar furniture finish.

SUNFLOWER AND MOROCCAN. Animate a casual or formal sitting area with a playfully painted accent piece. Introduce a small table into your decor if you are just beginning to decorate with painted furniture. (Small sizes are manageable as you learn painting techniques.) Experiment and stretch your creativity by hand-painting a design, by painting a tabletop in bright solids, or by painting a table base in neutral colors with bright accents. A base painted a dark neutral, such as taupe or black, and a brightly painted top with stylized stenciled motifs create a decorating statement that is uniquely yours.

◆ Painted with a powerful oversized sunflower design, a reproduction demilune-style pedestal table introduces cheerful colors into a sunroom setting, *right,* while the semicircle top contributes a pleasing shape to the square edges of the room. The height of the table is compatible with the arm of the rattan sofa, while the pattern and colors echo the energy of the floor pattern. **See page 88 for techniques.**

◆ Hand-painting strengthens the sunflower design, *below,* and relaxes a furniture style that is traditionally used in formal settings.

◆ Based on inlaid Moroccan mosaics, the painted tabletop, *left,* transforms a basic budget-priced pedestal table into a memorable work of art. Intricate designs such as this enrich the setting. **See page 86-87 for techniques.**

◆ A pair of antiqued reproduction French-style chairs share the painted mosaic table in a congenial grouping, *below.* The paisley fabric used to recover and update the chair seats and cushions enhances the rich color choices for the tabletop. Paisley and mosaic, merged with Asian-style pieces, offer a sophisticated and exotic setting in which the table becomes the focal point.

bedrooms

Revive dated furniture with fresh colors and themes that reflect your getaway fantasies.

◆ bedrooms

PARISIAN SKETCHBOOK. Free your imagination to fantasize about the bedroom of your dreams. For inspiration, give in to your image of an ideal place to live or vacation. For added guidance, spend time with memorable photo albums or glance through travel books, magazines, and websites of enticing, faraway places.

As you browse, visualize colors that soothe and calm you. On the practical side, consider which existing furniture has possibilities of taking on a more exotic life with paint and detailing. When you need to add furniture to your bedroom, shop for vintage or reproduction beds or chests that provide the qualities of charm and history while reflecting your travel longings.

◆ A summer vacation in Paris and the love for all things French meld into the idea for the palette and cheerfully stylized painted motifs, *right*. This project also updates two basic mid-20th-century family pass-along pieces. For lighthearted appeal, the bed and chest both feature the recognizable lively harlequin pattern in tints of lavender and apple green. The medium-tint lavender is repeated in the fresh and cool wall color, as well as in the detail on a previously stained bed. Making the definitive French accent, an artist has hand-painted sketches of the best known of all Paris landmarks—the Eiffel Tower. Three fleur-de-lis tiebacks, cut from plywood and hand-painted, support the bed hanging that matches the drapery panels. The result: a perfect retreat for an American in Paris.

See page 100 for techniques.

ROMANCE IN WHITE. Emulate the always chic white-on-white romantic presence with a carefully styled bedroom that minimizes color while emphasizing details. Turn to such a soothing scheme when your goal is to create a relaxing, composed retreat.

◆ Based on a vintage bed and armoire, both cleaned up and refreshed with paint, the bedroom, *above*, derives its charm from the color and pattern discipline. Carpet and bed linens contribute texture without a distracting, obvious pattern; the sheers soften and diffuse light while

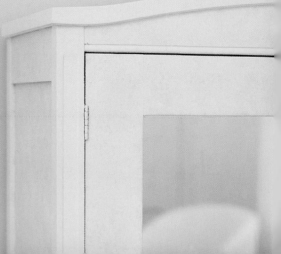

lending an ethereal atmosphere to the room. In keeping with the minimalist color approach, a painted pressed-tin fragment hangs above the bed, and a collection of oval platters artfully introduces diverse shapes. Silver-tone lamps pair with white silk lampshades, offering subtle contrast yet following the no-color rule. **See page 112 linen source.**

◆ Previously painted or antiqued furniture, such as the inherited armoire, *above left,* may require only cleaning and updated hardware to make a dramatic appearance in a room of painted furniture.

◆ A budget-stretching bookcase, *above right,* fits smartly into the chic setting courtesy of fresh white paint. It provides an ideal backdrop for a collection of old and new white vases, chosen for shapes and mixed with white-jacketed books. Books also can be covered with white paper, with artfully handwritten titles on the jacket spines.

◆ Previously antiqued, this handsome vintage bed, *left,* is revived with careful cleaning followed by touching up the detailing with paint. When furniture includes similar adornment, avoid multiple coats of paint that may obscure intricate motifs. **See page 89 for techniques.**

FOLK ART. An expanded interest in European styles translates into new reproduction furniture collections. Observe these pieces, *above,* to discover painted pieces that match your style. Rather than hold fast to only one furnituremaker, mix similarly finished pieces to achieve the one-of-a-kind look that comes from incorporating antiques and family treasures. Pair thrift store pieces with new or painted pieces. When you don't find the perfect country piece to complete your setting, create your own heirloom with paint and traditional motifs applied to a headboard, chest, or bedside table.

◆ The custom-designed headboard, *below and below right,* sports the most personal of motifs—a couple's hand-painted, combined monogram. Although a woodworking shop cut the featured headboard from ¾-inch plywood, an unfinished or secondhand store headboard would serve as well for this embellishment. A glazed finish over the painted headboard mellows the appearance and blends with the tones of the fern-printed fabric. Repeating the muted green found in the yellow-green tints of the print unifies the decorating scheme. The white coverlet and shams and the subtly striped sheets allow the painted and glazed headboard to play the starring role. As an alternative, one initial could be painted, or a monogram or an initial could be stenciled and softened with hand-painted accents. **See page 90 for techniques.**

◆ An antiqued, glazed finish rejuvenates a dated metal tray table, *right,* for a useful and attractive accent piece for a bath. The lip and the tray handles make the piece functional for grouping bath items and accessories. Small trays such as this also work well in the living room or family room as drink or magazine tables. Here, the muted colors and finishes echo the sophisticated tone of a white bath. Cutouts could also be decoupaged on the tabletop and sealed with polyurethane. **See page 89 for techniques. See page 102 for decoupaging.**

PATTERN ON PATTERN. Emulate popular pattern-on-pattern designer furniture that features whimsical motifs by initiating unique do-it-yourself painting projects. For the most fun and frolic, look for flea market pieces that have such detailing as turned legs, spools, spindles, or pressed backs that can be painted, papered, stenciled, or otherwise detailed.

◆ Trendy mixes stylishly with old-fashioned charm in this feminine, lively room, *opposite,* that could easily double as a one-of-a-kind guest room. The bed, decorated with floral wallpaper for the headboard, shows off a green-bordered skyscape for the footboard. The dramatic mix of hand-painted black and white checks combined with flower-centered diamonds contribute to the excitement. Gold balls enhance the now-interesting piece, *below right.* **See pages 96-97 for techniques.**

◆ An American country pressed-back chair, *above left and opposite,* takes on 21st-century style by way of a hand-painted country scene, a pink and white striped seat, and highlighted spindles. Decoupage offers an attractive alternative to hand-painting a scene. **See page 97 for techniques. See page 102 for decoupaging.**

◆ Paint plus pattern transform this narrow old-fashioned wardrobe into a design statement, *above right.* A marbleized paint finish introduces yet another pattern into the delightful mix. Gold-tone paint contributes a one-of-a-kind finishing touch.

RIBBONS AND ROSES. Create a room a young girl will grow into rather than out of. If you change accessories as the years pass, the delicately detailed painted furniture in this pastel room will charm her well into her teen years.

◆ A well-chosen paint scheme unifies and updates unmatched furniture, *above.* The single bed, dresser, and straight chair—all assorted flea market finds—appear made for the armoire, which was purchased unfinished. The secret to success is to work with pieces of similar scale and style and to repeat detailing and colors from piece to piece. Here, outlining with blue enlivens and coordinates the room without overpowering it. **See pages 102-103 for techniques.**

◆ Stripes on the walls, created with painter's tape, along with a painted peg rack, animate a room full of fresh pastels and youthful fabrics, *above and opposite.* Mixing pastels, patterns, cool blues and greens, tailored stripes, the lush bed hanging, and the chain-stitched floral rug conveys grown-up direction. The mosaic-framed mirror adds an exotic touch to the teapots, teacups, and floral plates.

◆ A hand-painted ribbon motif decorates the doors of the armoire, *above,* detailed with old-fashioned glass knobs. Stenciled motifs or wallpaper could be used as alternatives, or the doors could be painted to contrast with one of the colors used in the room. **See page 103 for techniques. See page 96 for wallpaper method.**

◆ Soft casual touches bring the scene together. Wide stripes on the lampshade, *left,* reflect the wall treatment. **See page 102 for techniques.**

OLD-FASHIONED GIRL. Give mismatched flea market or inherited furniture or flea market finds new life with an artful array of candy-box pastels. Recall the colors of dinner mints—and for the liveliest mix, collect paint chips of your favorite pastels plus white. Choose colors of the same intensity or degree of brightness—generally in corresponding locations on paint chips—to avoid a bright yellow, for example, overpowering a pale green.

◆ A patchwork quilt inspires the delicate pastel color scheme for this girl's room. The flea market lamp table goes from staid to lively with a bright white top and light yellow base, *right*. **See page 91 for techniques.**

◆ A dressing table, with applied detailing, is pretty in pink while the chair is lively in yellow and white, *below and below right.* White unifies the mix of pastels and pieces. **See page 91 for techniques.**

◆ The curved drawer fronts and scalloped apron of this early 20th-century chest lend themselves to the delicacy of soft green and white, *below left.* The white top introduces a crisp, contemporary air and repeats on each piece for pleasing design unity. Although this chest is an inherited family piece, look for similar ones at vintage furniture stores, flea markets, or tag sales. Older stained or painted pieces should be cleaned, repaired, sanded, and primed before painting in order for the paint to adhere. New hardware, such as these clear cut-glass knobs, *below,* purchased from a home furnishings catalog, stylishly updates vintage chests, dressing tables, desks, and wardrobes. In keeping with the pastel scheme inspired by a patchwork quilt, walls are washed in a soft blue as a backdrop for the painted furniture. The furniture trim allows each painted piece to stand out against the background. The coordinating decorative shelf displays a framed pastel print, while the small accent lamp, gingham lampshade, and a child's painted china tea set add pretty finishing touches to a room that will grow along with the little one. **See page 91 for techniques.**

RAVES FOR RICKRACK. As you search for fun and fresh starting points to decorate a girl's room, examine your sewing box for ideas. Instead of focusing on a specific motif or theme, consider trims and embellishments that could spark your imagination and color palette.

◆ Rickrack trim sets the stage for this bedroom, which features lilac, green, and yellow color blocks and stenciled trim, *opposite*. The repetition of colors and the rickrack motif between walls and furniture establishes the design focus for the cheerful setting. Painted stripes energize the headboard, which is detailed with stenciled rickrack. The rolling rickrack on the painted chest adds to the lighthearted fun, while a decorative discount store bracket, youthful flower power lamps, and color-themed bedding complete the scheme. **See pages 92-93 for techniques.**

◆ A child-size, pale green rocking chair, *above left*, acquires personality with stenciled rickrack and contrasting painted detailing. **See pages 92-93 for techniques.**

◆ Chosen for sturdy shape and finial-trimmed posts, the unfinished headboard, *above right*, displays the room's vibrant color palette. Unfinished or vintage headboards with detailing are effective for projects that involve contrasting paint colors.

◆ Shades of lilac attract interest to the drawer fronts, *right*, finished with white ceramic pulls. Deeper lilac is duplicated in the wide-stenciled rickrack that contrasts with yellow and green.

BRIGHT AND BOLD. Design your bedroom as a personal retreat with a one-of-a-kind custom bed crafted to your specifications. Create a palette of your favorite colors and patterns, and use appealing motifs on key furnishings.

◆ The custom king-size bed, *above,* sets the decorating theme, anchoring a large master bedroom decorated in an energetic rusty red and apple green palette. Because vintage or antique king-size beds are difficult to find, a custom investment like this may be worthwhile. The slightly distressed finish that gently ages the furniture is further softened with hand-painted flowers that embellish the massive headboard. The step stool, traditionally used with tall beds, coordinates with the bed and accents the room. The unified decorating scheme is achieved through red accents that repeat in the comforter, the painted back of the cupboard, and the plaid upholstery fabric.

◆ Paint, tape, and hand-painted detailing transform a standard desk, *right,* into an artful writing table. Paint outlines the slats of the ladder-back chair while hand-painted flowers provide added detail. As an alternative, floral motifs can be stenciled or stamped on one or more chair slats.

PLAY DRESS UP. Accentuate painted chairs with fabric and glued-on trim. Transform single chairs, often bargain buys at flea markets and secondhand stores, into dressing room or bedroom accents. Search for a mix of sturdy, paintable chairs in pleasing shapes and sizes. **See page 88 for techniques**

◆ Two originally dark and dowdy reproduction chairs, *left,* emerge clean and fresh with white finishes and flirty trims. Paired with a vintage pedestal table, also refreshed with white paint, the chair allure is further heightened.

◆ The chair skirt in a teen's study is gathered under a recovered seat to hide less-than-shapely legs, *below left.* Delicate flowers, stenciled on the slats, transform the chair from plain to pretty.

◆ The classic shape of the reproduction chair, *below right,* lends itself to a padded and trimmed velvet cushion worthy of Alice in Wonderland. Oversize tassels confer the fantasy finishing touch.

COWBOY HEAVEN. If the Old West feeds your child's sense of history and adventure, create the perfect home on the range (or ranch) with a fantasy bedroom. Use painted and decoupaged storage pieces as eye-catching focal points. Warm the cowboy-theme fabrics, accessories, and vintage finds with clever accessories that reflect your child's interests.

◆ A cowboy-motif rug and decoratively painted bricks set the stage for a crackle-drawer chest and a fire engine red cupboard, *below. and opposite.* Horseshoes, lone stars, hide-covered accessories, iron lamp bases, woven blankets, and a wagon wheel contribute to the appeal.

◆ The dark crackle drawer inset, *right,* imitates leather and contrasts with the light crackle finish. **See page 101 for techniques.** A reproduction cowboy-print fabric covers the invitingly comfortable chair.

◆ Decoupaged prints, *above and left,* add Old West scenes to the painted armoire, a vintage find. Decorative painting lightly ages the door and blends it with the painted walls. The cowhide-covered footstool looks at home in this room where furniture and accessories contribute to the theme while providing function. Jackets hang from rustic star hooks, well-worn cowboy boots present an organized display, and a refurbished trunk neatly stores toys. A new trunk, finished to look rustic with either a lighter-weight lid or opening side door, would be safer for little fingers.

◆ Classic Western adventures, such as the famous Lewis and Clark expedition, embellish the doors of the painted armoire, *left.* Art supply and crafts stores are good places to find prints and posters suitable for decoupaging. You can also stencil or stamp simple motifs.

See page 102 for techniques.

AROUND THE WORLD. Expand your child's horizons with a room inspired by cultures near and far. Rather than focusing strictly on one theme or country, create a backdrop for motifs, colors, and furnishings of diverse countries and continents. As a starting point, think about what countries and cultures are of particular interest to your child, perhaps those found in your family heritage, or a favorite school geography project. Look for existing furnishings that can be updated with paint, hardware, and detailing.

◆ Refreshed with black enamel, an iron metal bed anchors a room of exotic finishes and exotic furnishings, *above*. A faux zebra-skin rug repeats the effectiveness of black and white.

◆ With a nod to design influences from Native

American and Asian cultures, stylized geometric motifs detail the painted chest, *left*. Stained wooden knobs contrast with orange-red and white. **See page 94 for techniques.** The hammered silver mirror frame adds another exotic touch.

◆ Economical stock furniture provides the starting points for a wall unit and painted cupboard, *below,* that add much-needed storage for a busy student. Japanese characters are hand-lettered on the doors of the wall unit, painted black to match the bed. A hand-painted salamander crawls over the side and door of a striped tower cabinet. A salamander or other animal could be traced from a paper pattern and then filled in with paint. **See pages 94-95 for techniques.**

DINO AND MORE. If your child is a junior paleontologist, indulge this scientific interest with a room where the dinosaur reigns supreme. While these prehistoric creatures are enjoying an all-time popularity, it's easy to find bedding, accessories, and stencils. **See page 112 for sheet and comforter source.**

◆ Hand-painted to allude to geological layers, a basic plywood headboard fastens to the glazed green wall, *above right*. The headboard could be one color for a simple yet colorful treatment. **See page 98 for techniques.**

◆ Five of the headboard colors are repeated on the toy chest, which was purchased unfinished. The chest is further personalized with a stenciled and hand-detailed dinosaur, *below right*. **See page 98 for techniques and page 111 for stencil pattern.**

◆ The color scheme is also used to coordinate the sturdy child-size table and chair, *below*. A paint-wash technique is used for the surfaces, and dinosaurs are stenciled on the durable finished tabletop. **See page 98 for techniques.**

SEA AND SUN FUN. Little touches may be all it takes to imbue painted pieces with youthful style. Generous doses of white along with essential suggestions of favorite and fashionable colors can add lively accents. Paint or border placement is important, too, as it can effectively set off a painted piece.

◆ Based loosely on sailing under the open skies, the hand-painted border and painted chest work together in an inviting nursery setting, *left.* With motifs restricted to the border, the fashionable shades of yellow and periwinkle are also found in the chest. Chest feet and pulls contrast with the creamy white drawers and sides, while the top is decoratively hand-painted in a diamond design. **See page 99 for techniques.**

◆ The stylized diamond pattern is sketched with pencil, rather than tape, *below,* for the warm shades of yellow and orange that contrast with the cool blue. The moon-and-star bookends complement the wall border and provide finishing interest to the chest of drawers. **See page 99 for techniques.**

FLYING HIGH. Stimulate your baby's cognitive development with nursery adventures in the wild blue yonder based on primary colors. For the safest possible nursery, make sure the crib you select meets current safety requirements of slats no more than 2⅜ inches apart. Also, use paint formulated for child safety and follow the paint manufacturer's recommendations for application. **See page 111 for paint source.**

◆ With a globe-pattern rug setting the palette, the painted crib, *above,* restates the deep blue of the ocean. Commercial wall decals decorate the vibrant walls created with painter's tape and bright yellow paint. A wooden table, enlivened with stripes, contributes a patriotic touch. Moon-themed drapery panels, adorned with crescent-moon shapes, add the final detail. **See page 95 for techniques.**

◆ An unfinished dresser links the earth-and-sky theme after billowy white clouds are hand-painted over the deep, clear ocean blue, *below.* The paint, formulated for child safety, coordinates with the crib. Airplane pulls from a discount store are just the right finishing touch.

◆ To add valuable storage and vivid pattern to this high-energy nursery, an unfinished toy chest, *bottom left,* is painted, then accented with white and blue striped detailing to prevent an intense primary theme from overpowering a small room. Low, sturdy chests work well in a child's room. When a toddler is old enough to pick up toys, use lightweight pieces with easy lift tops for safety and convenience.

◆ The accent table, *below,* also purchased unfinished, replicates the All-American toy chest scheme. The retail lamp is a fortunate coordinating find. Repetition of color and detailing unifies this scheme while avoiding the chaos of furniture pieces that are too disparate. **See page 95 for techniques and page 112 for furniture sources.**

outside&in

Mix found treasures with painted furniture for inviting fresh-air living and dining spaces.

outside&in

EASY LIVING. Enjoy warm-weather relaxation in a screened porch with comfortable seating, pillows and throws, tables for drinks and snacks, and complementary art and accessories. Envision the porch as a comfortable retreat that makes the most of valuable space. Shop at secondhand and vintage furniture stores for painted and distressed furniture that add charm and age to the setting. Pair old or distressed pieces with new reproduction painted furniture or with unfinished pieces that you decide to paint. Highlight old pieces by cleaning them and touching them up as needed, letting their age define them. Use well-made vintage or secondhand furniture that can be repainted to suit your scheme or palette. In this most relaxed of all living and dining areas, introduce a medley of fragments and collections that you most enjoy.

◆ The timeless color combination of green and white reflects summertime fresh, as illustrated by this generously sized screened porch, *right.* An assortment of mismatched furniture, along with personal treasures, provides charming appeal. The settee's crisply tailored plaid seat cushion defines order and balance in the eclectic room. The gently worn finish of the vintage twig chair is a rustic accent for garden appeal. The green mid-20th-century-style wicker chair is enhanced with a coordinating floral pillow. The tongue-and-groove cabinet lends a rustic quality and provides always-needed storage. **See page 112 for shop sources.**

PORCH WITH PUNCH. Experience the power of paint with porch projects that transform the standard into the spectacular. For the most vibrant appeal and setting, paint the porch floor as well as a floor cloth. If you use the porch during the summer exclusively, add a small painted area rug for a finished, decorated look. Adapt color-block techniques by taping off and painting solid color blocks and diamond shapes. Include touches of black for sophisticated accents. Stencil commercial motifs that coordinate with your style, or craft your own stencils from room design elements. For an even simpler process, decoupage or stamp painted furniture and accent pieces with stylized floral or geometric designs.

◆ A combination of painting and stenciling embellishes a serviceable bench and a pair of ladder-back chairs in this entryway porch. Dramatic black and olive green anchor lively and fashionable violet and yellow accents in the bench seat. The trend of mixing patterns is

evident in the diamond pattern and stenciled cherries motif. **See page 110 for techniques.**

◆ The stenciled panels, framed by a painted border, recall botanical prints, *top right.* A floral print pillow and an architectural fragment complete the stylishly casual scene.

◆ Design interest is added with a diamond harlequin pattern on the seat, *right,* created with tape that allows the color and design of the stenciled cherry motif to stand out on the back of the bench.

FRESH-AIR LIVING. Enjoy your porch this summer which relaxed furnishings, such as painted and aged tables. Regard the porch as your warm-weather, expanded living space for easy and casual entertaining. Hang an old-fashioned porch swing in the mix for fun— it will quickly become the favored spot for reading, relaxing, and daydreaming.

◆ Created from a table base purchased from a used furniture store, the slightly distressed painted and scrubbed finish of the glass-top table, *right,* pairs new and old for fashionable dining. For a sleek look, the base could be primed and painted without the distressing. Smooth-edged tempered glass should be used for safety and durability. Glass rounds can be purchased at crafts and import stores or custom-cut at a glass shop. **See page 109 for techniques.**

◆ Lacy paisley motifs, accomplished with easy spray paint and stencils, decorate the top of the rustic plank coffee table, *below.* Such a quick technique would work equally well for a serving or display piece. **See page 109 for techniques.**

◆ Accessories such as the rustic birdhouse perched on the column, *left,* impart personality to a porch setting.

◆ Stock trim purchased from a home center details a stock porch swing, *below.* The unfinished porch swing is assembled, detailed with the trim, and sprayed with white paint for an easy interpretation of a classic Victorian-era swing. A light scrubbing provides the aged appearance. For a rustic look, the swing can be assembled without the trim, sprayed a dark green or barn red, and given a worn look with a light sandpapering. A previously painted wicker chair is refreshed with dark green paint to match the table base. **See page 107-108 for techniques.**

CHAIRS WITH PERSONALITY. Put a fresh new face and lighthearted spin on the classic porch rocker with a mix of four pretty pastels. Any porch rocking chair with slats will do for this project—including previously painted or stained chairs that are in sturdy and paintable condition. For added interest, look for chairs with ornate finials or other trim details that can be singled out for contrasting paint colors.

◆ On sunny, warm days these lively painted rocking chairs, *below*, migrate from the covered porch to the garden deck for neighborly conversation. The color scheme for each chair is based on one of the four pastels. **See page 104 for techniques.**

◆ Bands of trim are applied with a small artist's brush to detail the finials, *right*. The mix of color blocks and differing details from chair to chair contributes to the sense of festive, relaxing summertime fun.

◆ Paint and pattern, in a vibrant palette, unify three unmatched outdoor chairs and a cast-off table base into a patio-cafe-style setting, *above.* Hand-painting transforms chairs into art, while taping off yields precise lines to the stylized tabletop. **See page 85 for techniques.** A floorcloth, taped off and painted by the same artist, defines the setting with vibrant color block diamonds and the fluid movement of waves.

◆ The artist lightly pencils the sun-and-moon face on both sides of the painted folding chair, *left,* before painting the project. As one alternative, the moon face could be drawn and painted before the diamonds are filled in. Another alternative could be to paint the diamonds and then freehand-paint or stencil the moon, sun, or other motif over the diamonds. **See pages 106-107 for techniques.**

ADIRONDACK REVIEW. If you associate classic Adirondack chairs with pleasurably idle and long summer afternoons, enjoy these classics even more in creative combination colors and whimsical, clever detailing.

◆ Grasshoppers and dragonflies jump and flit across cobalt blue chairs. Stencil patterns are traced, cut from kraft paper, and reversed every other stencil. The insects are hand detailed in a loose and pleasing painterly style. Such accent chairs work well alone or in pairs.

See page 105 for techniques.

◆ What could be simpler than using two colors of green—a pleasing medium and a yellow green—to update these classic chairs and footrest? Shades of green in numerous variations from nature's own palette are always appealing in outdoor settings, *opposite*. For a pleasing effect, these greens contrast for definition but are within the same general intensity (brightness) to avoid one green from overpowering another. In a seaside environment, two shades of blue would be as effective. Clear medium blue, plus navy blue; or red, combined with a bright white would set a crisp nautical theme. **See page 105 for techniques.**

◆ Two deep greens, an olive and a clear medium, create color harmony with the plants and the terrace in a traditional formal garden, *above*. To reflect and capture the garden formality, the dark greens resonate the calm of the classic stonework and aged fragments in the handsome setting. Casual motifs and primary colors could look out of place in a garden where Old World style prevails.

The pairing of greens in the garden bench, however, offers an element of freshness and surprise to this classic outdoor furniture. Unadorned fabric pillows in contrasting and coordinating colors soften the hard lines of the bench and provide a welcoming sense of repose. As an alternative, the dark green used alone or a dark black green, like that seen in traditional shutters or porch rockers, would be an appropriate complement to the stonework garden setting. **See page 104 for techniques.**

decoratingideas

Painted furniture is fashionable and fun. A piece or two adds charm and personality to any setting, and a room brimming with painted pieces is a **classic design statement that has become fresh and new again.** Paint, preparation, and practice are all it takes to accomplish these wonders. Best of all, **projects can be as quick and easy or as intricate and creative as you want.** You can accomplish chic projects with variations of one color or the **simplest decorative painting techniques** such as sponging or ragging. You can employ fashionable color blocks—painting a piece or several pieces in different colors—for a no-fail update. If you would like to try detailed projects, paint allows you to create fantasy pieces, such as those based on a travel adventure, a child's special interest, or a faux surface such as mosaics. **Proper surface preparation is imperative for success.** Before beginning any of the featured projects, carefully read all of the instructions and gather the supplies listed. **Although featured projects start with either vintage (painted or stained) or unfinished pieces,** most projects will work as well for either. When you use vintage pieces, make sure they are in good repair. If the piece has been previously painted, you can sand and repaint in most

cases without stripping off old paint. You can also clean up and freshen previously antiqued furniture without having to strip it and start over. **In general, furniture requires sanding,** wiping with tack cloths or clean damp cloths to remove the dust, and priming to seal the finish. **These simple steps ensure clean,** paint-ready surfaces for the base coats and top coats. Some projects, however, incorporate the charm of the natural wood or previously stained wood for variations of the popular aged or antiqued effect. In those cases, directions may omit the primer. **Each project lists the paint name, type, finish, and special supplies to make it easy for you** to emulate the artist-tested projects. Also see the general supply list on page 78. More detailed project information is listed on page 111. You may prefer to have your paint custom-mixed at your favorite paint store or to use brands with which you are more familiar to create the color schemes of your choice. **The type of paint and the finish,** such as satin-finish interior latex

or artist's acrylic, **are important.** Exterior latex paint is used for some of the porch projects, for example, because of durability. Paint formulation and finish will affect the appearance and longevity of your projects. **Note that several projects are finished** with a recommended sealant, such as nonyellowing, water-based polyurethane. Use the artist-tested sealer for satisfactory results. Whether you use primer, sealant, or paint only, it's extremely important to allow complete drying between coats. **For best results, paint in thin coats and never rush drying times.** All materials in the supply lists, such as recommended brushes and masking tape, affect the quality of your work. When using spray paints or sealants, always work in a well-ventilated area with lots of fresh air.

Although stunning projects can be created using only paint or paint finishes, you'll find a number of projects that feature hand painting, stenciling, decoupaging, or glued-on trims. **Such detailing enriches and personalizes,** sometimes with surprisingly little effort. **Each project has complete directions** and includes how-to instructions both for working with commercial stencils and for making your own. Note the skill, time, and supplies. Use sources on page 112 to locate unfinished furniture as well as additional products and furnishings.

painted furniture projects

PAINTED FURNITURE BASIC SUPPLY LIST

Shop at crafts and art supply stores as well as home centers and paint stores for the specialty items needed for these projects. For unfinished furniture sources, see page 112. To make your project go as smoothly as possible, stock the following items in addition to the specific items listed with each project:

- Water- or oil-based primer
- Fine- and medium-grit sandpaper
- Steel wool in various densities
- Tack cloths and clean, lint-free cotton rags
- Blue painter's tape and low-tack adhesive tape
- No. 2 lead pencil
- Scissors
- Carbon, kraft, and tracing paper
- Level-ruler combination
- Straightedge and tape measure
- Stencil plastic and stencil brush
- Crafts knife and extra blades
- Cutting board or self-healing cutting mat
- Disposable foam plates and cups
- Repositionable spray adhesive
- 1- and 2-inch paintbrushes
- Assorted foam paintbrushes
- Plastic mixing bucket and containers
- Clear, matte-finish spray sealant
- Painter's drop cloth
- White chalk
- Cellulose sponge
- Portable hair dryer

PRINTS & PENGUINS

SKILL LEVEL
Beginner
TIME
2–3 days
SUPPLIES
- Latex enamel paint: white, green, salmon
- Artist's acrylic paint: black, white
- Small artist's brushes
- Nonyellowing polyurethane
- **Sources on page 111**

PRINTS & PENGUINS

(PROJECT SHOWN ON PAGES 4–7)

- **This project uses a sturdy, unfinished chest** with wooden pulls; it is also appropriate for a vintage chest. Lightly sand and prime for either an unfinished or a previously finished piece. Wipe with a tack cloth, prime, and allow to dry.
- **Paint with two coats of white enamel;** allow drying time after each coat. Plan the freehand designs on paper, sketching your ideas. Determine the width of the checks, using small artist's brushes. For the project, the drawer fronts are painted freehand in the two colors. If you prefer precise lines, measure and mark off lines with blue painter's tape.
- **Allow the drawer fronts to dry thoroughly.** Paint the animal motifs and drawer pulls freehand, as shown. If you prefer, stencil or stamp motifs and paint the pulls all one color or mix colors. (Paint in the colors used for the chest for a colorblock effect.) Allow paint to dry completely, at least overnight. Protect the surface with nonyellowing polyurethane.

FUN IN CALIFORNIA DINING CHAIRS
SKILL LEVEL
Beginner
TIME
2 days
SUPPLIES
- Wood stains: red, dark yellow, blue
- 2-inch nylon bristle paintbrush
- Matte-finish top coat
- Sources on page 111

TRANSFERWARE ARMOIRE
SKILL LEVEL
Intermediate
TIME
3–4 days
SUPPLIES
- Exterior satin latex paints: medium brown, dark brown, cream
- Artist's brushes
- Sources on page 111

FUN IN CALIFORNIA DINING CHAIRS
(PROJECT SHOWN ON PAGES 14–15)
- **This project uses unfinished wood chairs.** Sand the wood and remove the sanding dust with a tack cloth. Brush on one coat of stain in the desired color. Let the stain dry for 2 hours. (Depending on temperature and humidity, allow extra drying time.) Apply a second coat; let the finish dry. Brush on a matte-finish top coat; allow the finish to dry.
- **Sand lightly, remove the sanding dust with a tack cloth,** and apply a second coat of finish. This project mixes chairs finished with three different colors of translucent stain. If you prefer, choose one or two colors from the list or create your own combinations.

TRANSFERWARE ARMOIRE
(PROJECT SHOWN ON PAGE 18)
- **A collection of brown-and-cream transferware pottery** inspired the motif decorating this armoire. Determine that your armoire or cabinet is in paintable condition. Sand with fine- and then medium-grit sandpaper. Wipe with a tack cloth. Prime with a latex primer, and allow to dry.
- **Paint the base coat** medium brown. Let dry overnight. Paint a second coat cream. Allow cream paint to dry for about two hours. Use a medium-coarse steel wool pad and water to scrub off some of the paint, allowing areas of the base coat to show through.
- **Choose a simple stylized motif** from transferware or other pottery. Lightly draw on the design with a pencil. Using artist's brushes, paint designs with dark brown and cream. Allow to dry.
- **Mix brown paint with water in a 1 to 3 ratio.** Apply this color wash with a wide brush, brushing as the wash dries to prevent drips and runs. Allow to dry. With steel wool, rub areas to achieve an aged, worn look. Repeat the color-wash and rubbing process to achieve a pleasing effect.
- **Alternatives:** If you collect other colors of transferware, such as the popular blue and white, choose colors accordingly. Substitute creamy white and blue for the brown and cream. If you prefer, use commercial stencils for the hand-painted step.

DINING ROOM TABLE AND CHAIRS

SKILL LEVEL

Beginner

TIME

1–2 days

SUPPLIES

- Tan paint in eggshell finish
- Latex primer
- 1- and 2½-inch-wide gesso brushes
- Nylon scrub pad
- Terry cloth
- Clear paste wax
- **Sources on page 111**

SWEDISH CUPBOARD

SKILL LEVEL

Beginner

TIME

2–3 days

SUPPLIES

- Paint: gray, ivory
- Crackle medium
- Polyurethane
- **Sources on page 111**

DINING ROOM TABLE AND CHAIRS

(**PROJECT SHOWN ON PAGES 18–19**)

- **This project updates a vintage oak** dining table. The technique also could be applied to an unfinished table. Sand the table with fine- and then medium-grit sandpaper. Remove sanding dust with a tack cloth. Prime the table and allow the primer to dry.
- **Apply a base coat of** tan paint. On top of the base coat, apply a light even coat of primer with a 2½-inch-wide gesso brush, imitating wood grain with your brush strokes. Dry for 1 hour. Dampen a nylon scrub pad with water, and buff away areas of the off-white to reveal the undercoat. Allow to dry. Apply three coats of clear paste wax. Allow drying time after each coat.
- **For a more durable surface,** apply water-based polyurethane in place of wax.
- **The chair project uses unfinished chairs** that have a tight wood grain. Open-grain wood provides a different effect. (Try the technique on the bottom of the chair to determine whether you like the effect.) This technique is not suitable for previously painted chairs.
- **Apply a light coat of primer** with a 1-inch-wide gesso brush. Follow the grain of the wood to prevent brush strokes from showing. As soon as the primer dries, use water-dampened terry cloth to buff away portions of the primer to reveal the wood. Allow to dry thoroughly and apply two coats of clear paste wax.

SWEDISH CUPBOARD

(**PROJECT SHOWN ON PAGE 23**)

- **This project uses an unfinished cupboard. Practice first on a board.** Lightly sand the cupboard; remove dust with a tack cloth. Brush on the base coat over raw wood. Allow to dry.
- **Apply crackle medium,** following manufacturer's directions. Lightly brush on top coat of paint. Do not brush over or attempt to touch up the top coat. Doing so interferes with the crackling. Seal with polyurethane.

FRENCH BLUE AND WHITE KITCHEN TABLE

SKILL LEVEL
Beginner

TIME
2 days

SUPPLIES
- Satin latex paint: white
- Low-luster latex enamel paint: light blue, medium blue
- 3 medium-size natural sea sponges
- Clear, matte-finish spray sealant
- **Sources on page 111**

FRENCH BLUE AND WHITE KITCHEN TABLE
(PROJECT SHOWN ON PAGES 28–29)

- **This project uses** an unfinished table and chairs and a blue-and-white scheme. If you use a vintage painted piece, see directions on page 80 for preparing previously finished furniture. As alternatives, try red and white, green and white, or brown and cream.

- **Apply a base coat** of white. Let dry 6 to 8 hours. Apply a second coat and let dry. Pour about 1 cup of medium blue into a plastic container. Dip a natural sponge into the paint, dab off excess on a cloth, and lightly sponge across the tabletop. When the paint becomes sparse on the sponge, dip again, dab off, and continue sponging until table is covered. Let the top dry for 4 hours.

- **Create a soft color** by mixing one part light blue and one part white in a plastic container. Do not mix completely—allow some white and some blue to remain separate. Dip a fresh sponge into the mixture and repeat sponging process. Sponge paint randomly across the top of the piece so the bottom layer of color still shows through. This creates layers of texture and color. When the design is complete, let dry for 4 hours. Pour one cup of white into a clean container. Dip a fresh sponge into the paint, dab off excess, and lightly sponge over the blues with touches of white paint. The white paint should accent, not overpower, the blues. Let the paint dry for at least 4 hours.

- **When the tabletop is dry,** apply an edge around the side of the top, using a 1-inch foam brush and the medium blue. Work in long, sweeping motions to create a clean edge around the table. Let dry for 4 hours. Spray the tabletop with clear matte sealant and let dry for 4 hours. Reapply and let dry.

FRENCH BLUE AND WHITE CHAIRS
SKILL LEVEL
Beginner
TIME
2 days
SUPPLIES
■ Low-luster satin latex enamel paint: white, four shades of blue
■ Stencil brush
■ Commercial stencil
■ **Sources on page 111**

SWEDISH LINEN
SKILL LEVEL
Beginner
TIME
3 days
SUPPLIES
■ White shellac primer
■ Acrylic paint: blue
■ Water-based glaze
■ 3-inch brush
■ Sash brush
■ Commercial stencil
■ Clear, water-based, matte-finish sealer
■ **Sources on page 111**

FRENCH BLUE AND WHITE CHAIRS
(PROJECT SHOWN ON PAGES 28–29)

■ **This project uses unfinished** dining chairs. Sand and prime the chairs before applying the base coat.

■ **This project uses four varied** shades of blue paint. If you prefer, choose just one or two shades for your project. Refer to the accompanying table project for color combinations.

■ **Apply the first coat** of paint, choosing a different color for each chair. Let the paint dry on each chair for 6 to 8 hours. Apply a second coat; let the paint dry for 6 to 8 hours.

■ **Measure the center point of the back panel of the chair,** and position the stencil, using repositionable spray adhesive. Choose a commercial stencil with a fleur-de-lis or a similar stylized motif. Pour 3 tablespoons of white paint into a plastic container. Dip the stencil brush into the paint, dab off excess on a cloth, and firmly dab paint onto the opening of the stencil. Repeat the stenciling process for all chairs. Let the stenciled motif dry for 4 hours. Touch up chair paint as needed.

SWEDISH LINEN
(PROJECT SHOWN ON PAGE 22)

■ **This project uses an unfinished desk, which has been primed** with white shellac primer. Sand a stained desk, wipe with tack cloths, and prime with the white shellac primer. Allow to dry. Tint water-based glaze with blue acrylic. To create a subtle linen effect, horizontally brush on glaze. Allow to dry. Brush second coat of glaze in the vertical direction. Use a commercial stencil to detail as shown. **See previous project for stencil directions.**

■ **Seal with a clear sealer** in a matte finish.

BURLED AND AGED COFFEE TABLE

SKILL LEVEL

Intermediate

TIME

2–3 days

SUPPLIES

- Satin-finish, interior latex paint: black
- Light beige flat latex paint
- Commercially available translucent color glazes: reddish brown and medium brown
- Large color-washing natural-bristle brush
- Cheesecloth
- Nonyellowing, matte-finish polyurethane
- **Sources on page 111**

BURLED AND AGED COFFEE TABLE
(PROJECT SHOWN ON PAGES 20–21)

- **Read the directions completely** before starting this project. For best results, practice the technique, and test color choices on poster board. Paint legs, apron, and exterior of drawers with black interior latex paint. Allow to dry. Apply a second coat of black and let dry.
- **Tape off area painted black on** the underside of the coffee table, where the paint meets the unfinished underside edge.
- **To create the faux-burl-wood finish** on the top and underside of the coffee table, apply a base coat of beige paint. Allow to dry overnight.
- **Pour 1 cup reddish-brown glaze** into a plastic container; pour 1 cup medium brown glaze into a second plastic container. Dip a color-washing brush into the reddish-brown glaze and apply overlapping X-style strokes to the top of the coffee table. Continue applying X-style strokes until the glaze is completely removed from the brush. Redip the brush into the glaze, applying more overlapping X-style strokes. At the taped-off area, apply fresh glaze to the brush and brush a line of glaze to the taped edge. In a small X pattern, blend the newly applied glaze into the completed sections.

- **Using the medium brown, apply the second coat of glaze** before the first coat dries. Dip the brush into the medium brown glaze; apply overlapping X-style strokes as in the first coat. Blend the second glaze into the edges of the first glaze.
- **While the glazes are wet,** dab the table with cheesecloth rolled into a ball to soften the look and to remove obvious brush strokes.
- **Remove the tape within an hour** of completing the glazing. Allow the table to dry overnight. When the top surface is dry, apply two coats of clear matte sealant, allowing drying time after each coat.

AGED PATINA TABLE

SKILL LEVEL

Beginner

TIME

3 days

SUPPLIES

- Eggshell-finish, interior latex paint: white
- Crackle glaze
- Antiquing glaze
- Clear, matte-finish spray sealant
- **Sources on page 111**

ARTISTIC ARMOIRE

SKILL LEVEL

Intermediate

TIME

4–5 days

SUPPLIES

- Latex paint: white and red
- Acrylic paint: black
- Gold leaf paint
- Antiquing glaze
- Round artist's brush
- Small artist's brush
- Polyurethane
- **Sources on page 111**

AGED PATINA TABLE

(PROJECT SHOWN ON PAGE 21)

- **Lightly sand table.** Wipe with tack cloth. Apply white base coat and let dry 6 to 8 hours. If original table is dark wood, apply a second coat and let dry.

- **Apply crackle glaze,** following manufacturer's directions, and let dry for 6 to 8 hours. Apply a thin coat of antiquing glaze with a foam brush, allowing the crackle finish to show through. While the antiquing glaze is wet, wipe off excess glaze with a foam brush. Repeat this step to build up layers. Let table dry overnight.

- **Spray the entire piece** with spray sealant. Allow to dry. Repeat. Allow the table to dry for 48 hours before placing objects on it.

ARTISTIC ARMOIRE

(PROJECT SHOWN ON PAGE 26)

- **This project features an unfinished armoire, which was lightly sanded.** Seal with primer. Let dry overnight. Paint white for a dry-brush effect. Let dry 6 to 8 hours. Determine the size and placement of the diamonds, then draw them with a pencil and straightedge. Tape outside the penciled lines.

- **Using the red paint,** dip brush in glaze, then in red paint. Paint the diamonds. Hand-paint the other patterns with a round brush. After the red dries (2–4 hours), loosely paint designs over the red paint.

- **Add the black dots at the intersections** of the diamonds with an unused pencil eraser dipped in black paint. With a small artist's brush, outline the diamonds with the gold leaf paint. Allow piece to dry completely.

- **Rough up the edges with sandpaper** for a worn look; wipe with a tack cloth. Apply two coats of polyurethane; allow drying time between coats.

ARTISTIC ARMOIRE
SKILL LEVEL
Intermediate
TIME
3 days
SUPPLIES
- Oil-based stain: walnut
- Acrylic, semigloss enamel paint: sage green
- Hide glue
- Three 2-inch paintbrushes
- Airless sprayer (can be rented)
- Sources on page 111

FUN & FUNKY
SKILL LEVEL
Beginner
TIME
2 to 3 days
SUPPLIES
- Flat interior latex paint in bright colors: blue, red, orange, yellow, black, white
- ½-inch artist's brush
- Small artist's brush
- Satin-finish polyurethane
- Sources on page 111

ARTISTIC ARMOIRE
(PROJECT SHOWN ON PAGE 27)
- **Stain an unfinished cabinet** with an oil-based walnut stain. Don't prime before staining. Randomly brush hide glue over the cabinet, especially on areas of natural wear such as around doors. Let dry for 24 hours. Spray acrylic semigloss paint with airless sprayer. Smooth out paint with a paintbrush. Allow some paint to rub off piece.

FUN & FUNKY ROUND CAFE TABLE
(PROJECT SHOWN ON PAGE 71)
- **This project is constructed with an unfinished table top** and an existing table base. Sand lightly and apply two coats of primer. Compose design on paper and transfer to tabletop. Lightly draw the design onto the tabletop with a lead pencil. Apply blue paint with a ½-inch artist's brush, using short, multidirectional strokes to create a mottled effect.
- **Repeat with the** yellow, orange, and red paints. Paint in the center with white paint. Let dry for 2 hours.
- **Outline all the shapes** with black paint, using a small artist's brush. Let dry 4 hours. Apply three coats of polyurethane, allowing each coat to dry for 2 hours.

FRENCH BLUE AND WHITE SIDEBOARD CHEST

SKILL LEVEL

Intermediate

TIME

2 days

SUPPLIES

- Flat, interior latex paint: blue, white
- Furniture wax: dark brown
- **Sources on page 111**

MOROCCAN TABLE

SKILL LEVEL

Advanced

TIME

4 to 5 days

SUPPLIES

- Latex paint: red
- Acrylic paint: crimson, amber, aqua, blue, white, black, burnt umber
- Crackle glaze
- Two 2-inch paintbrushes
- Small artist's brush
- Watercolor brush
- Red pencil
- Water-based, satin-finish polyurethane
- **Sources on page 111**

FRENCH BLUE AND WHITE SIDEBOARD CHEST

(PROJECT SHOWN ON PAGE **28**)

- **This project uses a vintage sideboard.** Remove existing hardware. Lightly sand the entire piece. Wipe with a damp rag or tack cloth. Apply two coats of primer. Determine the size of the motifs by measuring the chest. Work out the pattern for your design on paper. Pencil in guidelines and then sketch the design freehand onto the chest.
- **Using the picture as a guide,** paint the chest, using blue and white paints. Let the paint dry. With white paint, dry-brush (use a brush with only the tips dipped into the paint) over the areas painted blue. Allow to dry overnight.
- **Sand the entire chest** with fine sandpaper for a worn and distressed look. Sand edges to expose the dark wood underneath. Wipe with tack cloth.
- **Wax the entire piece** with dark brown paste wax. Reattach hardware.

MOROCCAN TABLE

(PROJECT SHOWN ON PAGE **35**)

- **This project is created with a vintage table.** Sand with medium-grit sandpaper and wipe clean. Apply primer. Sand with fine-grit sandpaper. Wipe clean and paint entire table with two coats of red paint.
- **Draw the design.** Work out the details on paper before transferring to the painted tabletop. On tracing paper, draw a circle with a compass to equal the same size as the center field. Tape tracing paper to get the size you need.
- **Fold a quarter circle.** Fold the quarter circle into eighths, fold again in sixteenths to create a symmetrical eight-point star.
- **Open up the paper back to the quarter circle.** Use the three center folds of your paper as the guidelines. Working clockwise, measure 2½ inches down from the first and third folds. Use a straightedge and draw a line from the first mark to the edge of the circle on the folds to the right and left. Repeat for the second mark to make one-quarter of the star. Measure ¾ inch down from the star outline to repeat this design. Measure ⅜ inch from this line to draw the lines for the inner field of the star design.
- **Open the paper** one fold to the half circle. Turn the paper over and trace the quarter star design. Open for one half of the star. Turn the paper over and trace the half star to complete the whole star.
- **To transfer the design** to the tabletop, turn the drawing over, pencil side down. Center the circle with the center of the table. Transfer the design.

■ **To add the leaf design** to the outside points of the star, place a piece of tracing paper over one of the points. Make a drawing of the leaf on each side. Trace leaves at each point of the star on the tabletop. As an alternative, make a stencil for the leaf design. **See page 82 for stencil directions.**

■ **Mask off lines** with painter's tape to keep lines neat. With an artist's brush, paint the inner star with white acrylic paint. Rub the paint on the field with a brush to create a mottled effect that allows some of the amber to show through. Allow to dry. Mask off lines again to keep outlines neat. Paint the outer star with aqua acrylic paint, leaving the 3/8-inch band of amber between the white center field and the aqua star.

■ **Mix crimson** and blue for purple. If necessary, add a touch of black to shade or a touch of white to tint. Or use a tube of purple artist's paint. Paint the leaves with a watercolor brush.

■ **While the colors are drying,** create the inner design on the tracing paper star. Set the compass at 1/4 inch and make a half-inch circle at the center point. From the top (north) point of the star, draw a line to the bottom (south) point with a ruler and pencil. Repeat from the left.

■ **Place a piece of tracing paper** over the drawing, concentrating on the top (north) point and centerline. Sketch the red petal design, keeping the top point at the center. Curve the line down and out to the left. Curve sharply down to connect with the 1/2-inch circle at the center. Curve the right side up, out, and down; then curve sharply into two upper petals.

■ **At the middle of the upper petals,** draw an apostrophe shape pointing into the star point to the right of the design. The shape should be into, but not flush with, the edge.

■ **When you are satisfied with the shape,** trace the back side with a No.2 lead pencil. Turn the paper over and line up the design with one of the center lines on the original drawing. Trace this design on each line—north, south, east, and west.

■ **Trace this design onto** the white center field and paint the petals with red latex paint, making the windmill design. Keep the outline neat.

■ **Mix a dab of black** with blue acrylic paint to make dark blue. Paint the apostrophes with a watercolor brush. Allow the top to dry thoroughly.

■ **Following crackle glaze directions,** apply one coat to table base and tabletop border. When these are dry, apply one coat of red paint, brushing in one direction. Allow to dry.

■ **Protect the finish** with one coat of satin finish polyurethane. Let it dry.

■ **After the surface has dried,** mix burnt umber and black in a 3 to 1 ratio, so that the mixture appears more brown than black. Slightly thin the mixture with mineral spirits, and brush the mixture over the entire table. Wipe off excess, letting the pigment accumulate in carvings, grooves, cracks, and imperfections for a rustic look. Allow to dry. Finish with a coat of satin-finish polyurethane, allowing to dry. Sand with fine-grit sandpaper. Wipe with a damp rag. Apply the second coat of polyurethane.

SUNFLOWER TABLE
SKILL LEVEL
Intermediate
TIME
2 days
SUPPLIES
- Artist's acrylic paint: black
- Flat, interior latex paint: orange-red, egg yolk yellow, leaf green, lime green, red
- Artist's brushes
- Water-based polyurethane
- **Sources on page 111**

PLAY DRESS UP
SKILL LEVEL
Beginner
TIME
1 day
SUPPLIES
- Flat latex paint: white
- Staple gun
- Fabric scraps
- Hot-glue gun and glue sticks
- Beads and trims
- **Sources on page 111**

SUNFLOWER TABLE
(PROJECT SHOWN ON PAGE 34)
- **This project uses a reproduction table.** Lightly sand table with 100-grit sandpaper and wipe clean. Apply one coat of primer. Let dry for 1 hour.
- **Apply one** coat of orange-red paint to entire table. Let dry 2 hours.
- **Sketch design onto the table** with white chalk. Paint the petals, the spiral, and the band around the top with gold paint. Paint details on the base. Mix a little orange-red with the egg yolk egg paint to fill in the petals. Apply the leaf green paint over one edge of the spiral and paint a wave around the band. Use lime green to define the wave on the band. Outline the petals with red paint. Add details on the base as desired.
- **Let dry** 4 hours.
- **Mix a small amount** of black acrylic paint with water to create a thin wash. Brush this over the entire piece to give an antiqued look. Let dry.
- **Apply three coats** of polyurethane, allowing at least 2 hours drying time between each coat.

PLAY DRESS UP
(PROJECT SHOWN ON PAGE 53)
- **This project uses a collection of vintage chairs.** Remove chair seat. Wrap the seat with your choice of fabric; set aside. Lightly sand the chair, prime, and brush on white paint. Work in a loose manner so the chair looks distressed.
- **Allow to dry.** Replace chair seat. Attach beads and trim with a hot-glue gun.

**ROMANTIC WHITE
BEDROOM
SKILL LEVEL**
Beginner
TIME
2 to 3 days
SUPPLIES
■ Semigloss latex paint:
white
■ Artist's acrylic paint:
raw umber
■ Clear paste wax
■ **Sources on page 111**

**FOLK ART TRAY TABLE
SKILL LEVEL**
Intermediate
TIME
2 days
SUPPLIES
■ Decorative paint: olive
■ Decorative metallic
glaze: bronze, gray
■ Color-washing brush
■ Cheesecloth
■ Clear, matte-finish
spray sealant
■ **Sources on page 111**

ROMANTIC WHITE BEDROOM
(PROJECTS SHOWN ON PAGES **40–41**)

■ **This project refreshes** previously antiqued
vintage furniture without stripping. The
directions also can be used to renew previously
painted furniture. To refresh antiqued furniture
that looks worn or discolored, clean with a
general purpose cleaner. Allow to dry.

■ **Thin semigloss latex paint** in a 1-to-1 ratio
with water. Rag over the surfaces with a soft,
clean cotton cloth. Allow to dry. Paint details
with interior semigloss paint. Allow to dry.
Thin raw umber artist's acrylic paint and rub
it into recessed areas for an antiqued effect.
Wipe away excess with a clean rag. Finish
with a coat of clear paste wax or water-based
polyurethane.

■ **Add unfinished pieces to blend** with the
refreshed antiqued pieces. Sand and prime
the bookcase, or other unfinished piece, and
paint with satin latex paint.

FOLK ART TRAY TABLE
(PROJECT SHOWN ON PAGE **43**)

■ **This is an ideal project to revive** an aged
wooden or metal tray table. Sand peeling paint,
if painted, and wipe with tack cloths. Apply
appropriate wood or metal primer before
applying the base coat.

■ **When the primer is dry,** brush on the olive base
coat and let dry 4–6 hours. When the top of the
tray is completely dry, turn over and paint
underneath with the olive base coat and allow to
dry. If painting a metal tray, expect quicker drying
time than a wood tray. (An unfinished wood tray
will need a second coat.)

■ **Pour about 1 cup** of the bronze metallic glaze
into a plastic container. Dip the end of a color-
washing brush into the glaze and apply to the top
of the tray, using quick X-style strokes. While the
glaze is wet, dab with dry cheesecloth to create a
mottled effect. Allow to dry about 3 to 4 hours;
turn the tray over, and repeat on the underside of
the tray. Allow to dry.

■ **Pour about 1 cup** of gray metallic glaze into a
plastic container. Brush on the gray glaze with
quick X-style strokes. Dab with dry cheesecloth.
Let dry 4 to 5 hours; repeat on the underside of
the tray. Let the tray dry.

■ **Apply two coats of spray sealant.** Allow sealant
to dry after each coat.

FOLK ART
MONOGRAM
HEADBOARD
SKILL LEVEL
Intermediate
TIME
2 days
SUPPLIES
■ Interior satin latex
paint: grass green,
cream
■ Antiquing glaze: gray
■ ⅜-inch artist's brush
■ Green lead pencil
■ Wood glue
■ Clear, matte-finish
sealant
■ Sources on page 111

FOLK ART MONOGRAM HEADBOARD
(PROJECT SHOWN ON PAGE 43)

■ **This project is created with a custom-made, unfinished headboard** and stock finials, which are attached with wood glue. Apply one coat of grass green and allow to dry. Apply second coat and allow to dry.

■ **To place the monogram,** measure the horizontal and vertical center of the headboard. Mark the intersecting spot with a pencil.

■ **Using this center point as a guideline,** draw the large monogram freehand. Note how the center point falls in the middle of the center letter. Pencil small initials on each side. Finish the design with freehand scrolls.

■ **Using a ⅜-inch artist's brush,** paint the monogram cream. Let dry for 6 hours. Apply antiquing glaze with a 2-inch brush in quick, broad strokes across the headboard. Immediately rub off the glaze with a clean foam paintbrush, using the same broad strokes.

■ **When the entire headboard** has been painted with the glaze-and-wipe technique, repeat the glazing process twice more. Paint and glaze the top and sides of the headboard.

■ **After you achieve the desired aging,** let the headboard dry. Seal with clear matte sealant.

■ **As an alternative,** stencil the monogram with commercial stencils, varying the sizes for interest. If you find a lettering style you like, enlarge it on a photocopier to make a stencil. Follow the stenciling directions on page 82. Another variation is to decoupage your motif, following the decoupage directions on page 102.

OLD-FASHIONED GIRL'S ROOM
SKILL LEVEL
Beginner
TIME
4–5 days
SUPPLIES
- Acrylic paints: soft green, pink, pale yellow, white
- Clear, satin-finish polyurethane
- Glass pulls
- **Sources on page 111**

OLD-FASHIONED GIRL'S ROOM
(PROJECTS SHOWN ON PAGES **48–49**)

- **This project brightens and updates** mismatched pieces of vintage furniture. If you purchase vintage or flea market furniture for such a project, shop for pieces with interesting shapes and detailing, such as the tall chest and dressing table. Don't be deterred by dark stains or chipped paint. With proper preparation, most pieces can be revived for a youthful look.

- **Choose colors that coordinate with** existing wall colors or fabrics in the room. An heirloom quilt provides the inspiration for this room. Remove hardware from chests and vanities. Sand first with medium- and then fine-grit sandpaper. Remove sanding dust with a tack cloth. Prime all surfaces with stain-blocking primer sealer, and allow the paint to dry thoroughly.

- **Paint the surface colors** as shown. Brush on a base coat with long smooth strokes to ensure a smooth finish. Recoat if necessary, allowing drying time between the coats. (Warm, dry days are ideal for painting. The more time between coats, the more durable the finish.) When the base coat is dry, paint the tops of each piece.

- **After each piece is completely dry,** seal with nonyellowing, satin-finish, clear polyurethane. Allow to dry. Reattach original hardware or affix new pulls.

RAVES FOR RICKRACK
SKILL LEVEL
Intermediate
TIME
3 days
SUPPLIES
- Interior latex paint: lemon yellow, light lilac, dark lilac, light pastel green, dark pastel green
- Tube of white crafts paint
- 2-inch tapered brush
- No. 10 round brush
- Artist's detail brush
- Green and purple pencils
- T-square
- Rickrack stencil
- Stamps: daisy in two sizes
- Clear, matte-finish polyurethane
- **Sources on page 111**

RAVES FOR RICKRACK

(PROJECTS SHOWN ON PAGES 50–51)

- **This project** features a custom unfinished headboard and an unfinished nightstand and rocker. Vintage furniture can be substituted.
- **Sand the surfaces** with fine-grit sandpaper and remove the dust with a tack cloth.
- **Prime the headboard** and allow to dry. Paint the body of the headboard and the finials light green. Paint posts yellow. Allow to dry. Apply second coat if necessary. Allow to dry.
- **Measure the distance** between headboard posts, and calculate the number of 4- to 5-inch-wide stripes that will fit between the posts. With the green pencil and a T-square, draw vertical lines along the headboard. Alternately paint the stripes in the two shades of green. Use a straightedge and the purple pencil to draw vertical lines down the center of each green stripe. Hand-paint the lilac stripes with an artist's detail brush. Hand-paint lilac detailing around the top of each finial.
- **Sand the nightstand** with medium- and then with fine-grit sandpaper. Wipe with a tack cloth. Prime the top, sides, and bottom panel yellow; paint the legs light green.
- **Paint the drawer fronts.** Create a checkerboard effect by painting the drawer fronts two shades of lilac
- **Detail the top.** Stamp daisies in white using two sizes of commercial stamps. Allow to dry. Stamp again in lilac, slightly outside the first stamped lines.

■ **Sand the rocking chair** with fine-grit sandpaper.
Wipe clean with a tack cloth. Base-coat the chair
light green and allow to dry. Apply a second coat
of green. Paint the tops of the rocker arms lilac.
Hand-paint details with an artist's brush.

■ **Make the rickrack stencil.** To make your own
rickrack pattern, purchase rickrack the size you
desire. Spray a section of trim with repositioning
spray adhesive and arrange on paper. Trace onto
paper, then transfer to stencil plastic and trace
again. Cut out the stencil with a crafts knife on a
self-healing cutting board to avoid damaging
surfaces. Leave ¾ inch of the stencil plastic
above the design to help maintain an even space
between the edge of the furniture and the
pattern.

■ **Stencil the rickrack lilac.** Affix a 4-inch section
of the stencil with repositionable spray adhesive
to the furniture surface. Adjust the stencil as
needed along the headboard, dresser, and rocking
chair to complete the design, using the corner
stencil to turn corners.

■ **Allow the painted surfaces to dry** at least 2
days. Seal with matte-finish clear polyurethane.

AROUND THE WORLD DRESSER
SKILL LEVEL
Intermediate
TIME
4–5 days
SUPPLIES
■ Shellac primer: white
■ Exterior flat latex paint: brick red
■ Artist's acrylic paint: white
■ Commercial stencils
■ One-step stain and sealer: walnut
■ **Sources on page 111**

AROUND THE WORLD STORAGE UNIT
SKILL LEVEL
Intermediate
TIME
4–5 days .
SUPPLIES
■ Oil-based, semigloss paint: black
■ Artist's acrylic paint: white
■ No. 6 filbert brush
■ **Sources on page 111**

AROUND THE WORLD DRESSER
(PROJECT SHOWN ON PAGE 57)
■ **This project uses a vintage dresser.** Remove the pulls and sand the dresser surface with fine-grit sandpaper. Wipe with a tack cloth. Prime the dresser with white shellac. Allow to dry. Brush on two coats of red latex paint. Allow to dry between coats.
■ **Position the stencils** with repositionable spray adhesive. Use white artist's acrylic paint and a round stencil brush to stencil the design. The paint will appear bright. Allow the stencil paint to dry, then achieve an aged look by wiping the chest and pulls with one-step stain sealer. Attach pulls when the finish is dry.

AROUND THE WORLD STORAGE UNIT
(PROJECT SHOWN ON PAGE 57)
■ **This project uses unfinished, inexpensive stock** storage units. Sand with fine-grit sandpaper, wipe clean with a tack cloth, and prime the cabinet. After the primer dries, brush on three coats of black oil-based paint. Choose words or characters that represent happiness or good luck, enlarging the characters on a photocopier to the size you prefer. Cut out the characters, and use repositionable spray adhesive to attach them to the cabinet. Trace around the characters, remove them, and fill in the outlined area with white acrylic paint, using the No. 6 filbert brush. As an alternate choice, you can paint freehand designs.

AROUND THE WORLD TOWER CABINET

SKILL LEVEL

Intermediate

TIME

3–4 days

SUPPLIES

- Semigloss interior latex paint: red, pale yellow, medium yellow
- Artist's acrylic paint: black, purple, dark yellow
- 1-inch flat and No. 8 round brushes
- Clear satin latex polyurethane
- **Sources on page 111**

FLYING-HIGH NURSERY

SKILL LEVEL

Beginner

TIME

4–5 days

SUPPLIES

- Acrylic spray paints intended for use on children's furniture: primer, red, white, blue
- **Sources on page 111**

AROUND THE WORLD TOWER CABINET

(PROJECT SHOWN ON PAGES 56–57)

- **Sand and prime the unfinished cabinet.** Allow the primer to dry. Paint all surfaces pale yellow. Allow to dry. Measure and then tape off 3-inch vertical sections with painter's tape. Paint alternate stripes with medium yellow.
- **Paint the salamander** design freehand or draw the design on a large sheet of paper, cut out, and trace onto the cabinet. The stylized salamander is painted as though it were crawling up the cabinet. Working with 1-inch flat and No. 8 round brushes, paint the salamander red. Outline with black acrylic and add black spots and purple eyes. Paint a stylized sun motif, using the dark yellow, on the arch of the cabinet door.
- **Allow to dry thoroughly.** Seal with clear satin latex polyurethane.

FLYING-HIGH NURSERY

(PROJECT SHOWN ON PAGES 60–61)

- **This project uses new unfinished furniture. (See page 112 for sources.)** If you use older furniture, make sure the crib meets current safety standards. Slats should be no wider than $2\frac{3}{8}$ inches apart to prevent a baby's head from becoming entrapped. If you use previously painted or stained furniture, sand with fine-grit sandpaper and wipe with a tack cloth before priming to ensure that the finish adheres. This project uses primer and paints that are safe for use on children's furniture and toys.
- **Sand, wipe the pieces with a tack cloth,** and prime the unfinished pieces. Allow the primer to dry. Follow the paint manufacturer's directions and work in a well-ventilated area, shaking and swirling cans to properly mix the paint. This water-based paint differs from other spray paints and requires practice to achieve an even coat.
- **For hard-edge surfaces,** such as the edge of the small table, mask with blue painter's tape before painting.

PATTERN-ON-
PATTERN ROOM
SKILL LEVEL
Advanced
TIME
4–5 days
SUPPLIES
■ Spray white shellac
primer
■ Artist's acrylic paints
in 20-ounce bottles:
dark green, sage
green, creamy yellow,
light blue, raspberry,
white, dark brown,
gold, black, light
purple
■ White gesso
■ Black artist's acrylic
■ No. 8 round brush
■ 1-inch flat brush
■ ¼-inch flat brush
■ ½-inch flat brush
■ No. 6 filbert brush
■ No. 2 fine brush
■ No. 5 round brush
■ 1 roll of wallpaper
■ Clear, satin finish
latex varnish
■ Sources on page 111

PATTERN-ON-PATTERN ROOM
(PROJECTS SHOWN ON PAGES 44–45)

■ **The three featured projects in this room** are created from the combined supply list, using 20-ounce bottles of artist's acrylic paints. A detailed armoire enhances the pattern mix. Five patterns are combined with solid colors and pattern wallpaper for this lively mix.

■ **Plan a balanced pattern arrangement.** Repeat patterns and use them in varying scales for visual impact.

■ **Sand, wipe with a tack cloth, and prime all surfaces to be painted.** Sand again lightly and wipe with a tack cloth. **Refer to the photos, above and on pages 44–45, for patterns.** At the top of the armoire, paint a rainbow stripe in raspberry and light purple, thinned with white gesso. While the paint is wet, slightly blend the two colors with a 1-inch flat brush to soften the color transition.

■ **Allow the rainbow stripe** to dry. Mix light blue and white to paint the sky area, blending slightly to allow variations in tones. Add a touch of pink (combine white and raspberry) and creamy yellow to keep it from looking flat. Paint the background with a ½-inch flat brush. Allow to dry. Dab on clouds using a No. 6 filbert brush and white gesso. Shade clouds with gray made by mixing a small amount of black with gesso.

■ **Create the confetti border.** Dot the colors randomly with a No. 8 round brush, one color at a time, over the entire area. The colors used in this project are light purple, light blue, creamy yellow, sage green, and raspberry.

■ **Paint the check pattern.** Using the No. 6 filbert brush, paint freehand black checks over the white base. Add an occasional streak of raspberry in some of the black checks for interest. Allow to dry.

■ **Paint the marble effect.** Use sage and dark green with a little creamy yellow to paint a mottled background, blending the edges of the colors to create a range of lights and darks. Mix dark brown with a little raspberry, and use the mixture with a No. 2 fine brush to add marbled veins, feathering the veins over the green background.

■ **Paint the door** wet on wet, using raspberry paint and white gesso. Blend the paints minimally to achieve a mottled effect. Outline the inner edge of the door with dark green. Trim the edges of the side panels and the bottom of the checked trim with gold.

■ **Apply floral wallpaper** to the side panels. Seal the cabinet with clear satin-finish latex varnish.

PATTERN-ON-PATTERN CHAIR

■ **This project uses a vintage** pressed-back chair.
Lightly sand and wipe with a tack cloth. Spray on
a coat of white shellac primer. Allow to dry.

■ **Dilute raspberry and light blue** acrylic paints
with water. Using a 1-inch flat brush, stripe the
seat. Strive for a streaky, not smooth, effect.
Using a No. 8 round artist's brush, detail the
spindles and stretchers with raspberry, light
purple, and gold.

■ **Following the armoire directions,** paint the
confetti design on the bottom portion of the chair
legs. On each stile, paint the check pattern with
a ¼-inch flat brush; paint the stile cap gold.

■ **Dilute sage green and brush lightly** over the
chair splat. Allow to dry. For this project, an artist
painted a landscape in the center of the splat.
Alternately, use a color photocopy or decoupage
an image from an art magazine. (See page 102
for more on decoupaging.) Allow the chair to dry,
and seal with satin- finish latex varnish.

PATTERN-ON-PATTERN BED

■ **Wallpaper the headboard.** Use an unadorned
headboard. Sand all surfaces, wipe with a tack
cloth, and spray with white shellac primer. Paper
the flat surface of the headboard. Trim with
raspberry paint lightened with white gesso. Detail
the inner edge with dark green. Detail the top
edge of the headboard with diamond patterns and
gold dots.

■ **Decorate the footboard** with a combination of
the sky and the check patterns, following the
armoire pattern directions. Use the ½-inch flat
brush for the check pattern. Paint the finials
gold. Using a No. 2 fine brush, paint a diamond
pattern in purple on the footboard bed posts.
Paint gold dots, using a No. 5 round brush, in the
center of each diamond. Repeat raspberry border
edged in dark green on the footboard. Seal with
satin finish latex varnish.

SKILL LEVEL

Intermediate

TIME

3 days

SUPPLIES

- Acrylic latex paint: red, pale green, navy, lilac, yellow, orange
- Small tube of forest green crafts paint
- Paint marker: black
- Decorator's glaze
- 2-inch tapered brush
- White candle for waxing
- Nonyellowing, matte-finish polyurethane
- **Sources on page 111**

DINO AND MORE

(PROJECTS SHOWN ON PAGE 58)

- **These projects use stock unfinished furniture.** All pieces are sanded and primed before painting.
- **Paint the headboard pale green.** Allow to dry. With a 2-inch tapered brush paint multicolored horizontal waves, referring to the photo on page 58. Waves don't have to be opaque; allow some of the pale green to show through. Add narrow forest green waves; detail them with vertical dashes. Allow to dry. Lightly sand the headboard with fine sandpaper. Wipe clean with a tack cloth. Seal with matte finish, nonyellowing polyurethane.
- **Paint the toy chest** with one coat of pale green. Allow to dry. Wax the edges. Paint the inside navy, the lid red, the front orange, and the front bottom blue, as shown. The sides remain pale green. Allow to dry. Lightly sand the chest, and wipe with a tack cloth.
- **Apply the dinosaur stencil** on the front center of the chest. Using repositionable spray stencil adhesive, stencil the dinosaur body lilac and the dinosaur spines red. Allow the paint to dry. Detail the dinosaur with a black paint marker and add hand-painted yellow spots. Allow to dry. Seal with matte-finish, nonyellowing polyurethane.
- **Paint the chairs** pale green. Allow to dry. Rub a candle onto the edges and in streaks, going with the grain of the wood. Do not wax the legs and spindles.
- **Brush a thin layer of navy paint** onto the chair seats. Brush a thin layer of orange on the splat across the top of the chair. Allow to dry. Sand with fine-grit sandpaper and wipe clean. Paint will sand easily from areas streaked with wax, revealing the green base. Detail the chair seats and slats with red and green paint. Allow to dry.
- **Paint the table pale green.** Allow to dry. Use the candle wax technique on the tabletop in the same manner as the chairs. Paint the top navy. Allow to dry. Sand with fine-grit sandpaper to remove some of the navy. Wipe with a tack cloth. Detail as shown. Add the stenciled dinosaur or a design of your own. **(See page 111 for stencil pattern and page 82 for stencil directions.)**

SEA AND SUN CHEST OF DRAWERS

SKILL LEVEL

Intermediate

TIME

1 day

SUPPLIES

- Flat interior latex paint: red, orange, yellow, green, blue
- ½-inch artist's brush
- Polyurethane
- **Sources on page 111**

SEA AND SUN CHEST OF DRAWERS
(PROJECT SHOWN ON PAGE 59)

- **Lightly sand the top,** pulls, and feet of a white painted chest. Wipe with a tack cloth. Apply primer to the sanded areas. Let dry 1 hour. With a pencil, lightly sketch the squares on the top of the chest. Using a ½-inch artist's brush, fill in the design with the yellow, orange, and green paints. Apply with short, multidirectional brush strokes for a mottled effect. Let dry 1 hour. Paint the dresser top border, outline the painted squares, and paint the dresser feet red. Paint the drawer pulls blue. Let dry for 2 hours. Apply three coats of polyurethane over the newly painted areas, allowing each coat to dry before applying the next.

PARISIAN SKETCHBOOK BEDROOM

SKILL LEVEL

Advanced

TIME

4 days

SUPPLIES

- All-purpose cleaner
- Flat latex paint: white
- Acrylic latex paint: yellow green, pink, lilac, blue, black
- Artist's round brush
- Flat sponges
- Matte-finish polyurethane
- **Sources on page 111**

PARISIAN SKETCHBOOK BEDROOM
(PROJECTS SHOWN ON PAGES **38-39**)

- **This project is based on a** '40s-style bed and dresser. Clean both pieces with a diluted all-purpose cleaner. Sand with fine-grit sandpaper, and wipe with a tack cloth. Apply a coat of stain-blocking primer/sealer. Allow to dry. Base-coat all pieces with flat white latex paint.
- **Dresser.** Choose a diamond size based on the size and scale of the dresser, referring to the photograph for scale. Cut a paper template of the diamond shape and trace it onto a sponge. Cut out the shape. Practice sponging the diamond on scrap paper. With a No. 2 lead pencil, lightly draw a line down the center of the dresser. Begin sponging at the top drawer, centered over the pencil line. Continue to sponge down the center line of the dresser. Using the photo as a guide, continue the process of sponging, using the additional colors and leaving a space between diamonds. Paint remaining areas of dresser as shown in photo.
- **Cut out stylized flowers from sponges** with a crafts knife. Dip the sponge into pink paint. Sponge the top of the arch on the dresser top. Allow to dry.

- **Lightly sketch the Eiffel Tower,** squiggles, and words in pencil. Using an artist's round brush, paint with black paint.
- **Bed.** Use the same supplies and techniques as for the dresser. Measure and mark the center of the headboard with a pencil. Make a diamond-shape sponge and, referring to the photograph, begin sponging down the center. Sponge along both sides, leaving space between the diamonds.
- **Sponge the flowers on the footboard** and on the center of the headboard. Paint solid colors as shown in photo on the headboard and footboard of the bed. Lightly sketch and paint details, following the instructions for the dresser.
- **Seal all pieces** with two coats of matte-finish polyurethane.

**COWBOY HEAVEN
DRESSER
SKILL LEVEL**

Intermediate

TIME

3 days

SUPPLIES

- Flat or satin latex
paint: black, off-white
- Acrylic paint: burnt
umber
- Crackle sizing or
medium
- Latex glazing liquid:
1 quart
- 6-inch foam roller
and covers
- Paint trays
- Clear, matte-finish
acrylic spray finish
- Sources on page 111

COWBOY HEAVEN DRESSER
(PROJECT SHOWN ON PAGE 54)

- **This project uses a previously painted dresser.**
Remove the drawers from the dresser and remove
the drawer pulls. Sand all dresser surfaces with
fine-grit sandpaper; wipe with a tack cloth.
- **Apply a coat of crackle sizing** to the dresser
with the foam roller, making sure not to drip the
medium. Use a foam brush for hard-to-reach
places. Let the medium dry until no longer tacky
to the touch. Apply a second coat of crackle
medium. Discard the roller cover. When the
second coat is no longer tacky (1-2 hours), pour a
generous amount of off-white paint in the roller
tray. Saturate foam roller with paint and apply a
heavy layer to the dresser top.
- **Roll in one direction** to the edge of the dresser
in one smooth motion. Add more paint to the
roller and roll a second roller width, making sure
the edges line up but do not overlap. (Rolling
over previously painted areas will lift the paint
from them, interfering with the crackling
process.) Repeat this process for the sides and
front of the dresser. Allow to dry for 24 hours.
Paint will crackle on its own. Repeat the
crackling process on the drawer fronts, except for
where the black paint is applied. (Here as the
center ovals.) The black paint can be applied
with a roller or a small foam brush if it is
narrower.
- **After the dresser and drawers have dried** for at
least 24 hours, mix 1 cup of the glazing liquid
with 1 tablespoon of burnt umber paint. Pour the
mixture into a clean roller pan. Roll the mixture

onto a small section of the top of the dresser.
Blot with a clean rag to remove some of the
glaze. Do not blot the edges of the wet glaze; you
must roll the next section of glaze next to this wet
edge and then begin blotting the seam to blend
the two sections so that no roller line is apparent.
Continue this process on the entire piece. Allow
to dry for about 8 hours. Spray with 2 coats of
clear matte sealant for protection. Allow to dry
completely between coats.

**COWBOY HEAVEN
ARMOIRE
SKILL LEVEL**
Beginner
TIME
1 day
SUPPLIES
- Images to photocopy
and decoupage
- Foam paintbrush
- Decoupage medium
- Sources on page 111

**RIBBONS AND ROSES
GIRL'S LAMP
SKILL LEVEL**
Intermediate
TIME
1 day
SUPPLIES
- Paint: same as
armoire project on
page 103
- 1-inch flat brush
- ½-inch flat artist's
brush
- Small, round brush
- Liner brush
- 1 wooden lamp
painted white
- 1-inch plain white
shade
- Sources on page 111

COWBOY HEAVEN ARMOIRE
(PROJECT SHOWN ON PAGE 55)

- **This project uses a painted armoire** with paneled doors. Images can be found in art books, such as those about Frederic Remington. Size images to fit the panels. Apply a generous coat of decoupage medium to a door panel with a foam paintbrush. Carefully place the image on the panel, making sure there are no wrinkles. Gently smooth out any bubbles. Allow to dry (about ½ hour). Apply a coat of decoupage medium on top of the image.

- **Continue adding layers of decoupage medium** until you can no longer feel the edge of the photocopied image; it may take four to five coats. Allow to dry completely between each coat.

RIBBONS AND ROSES GIRL'S LAMP
(PROJECT SHOWN ON PAGE 47)

- **Divide the shade into four equal sections,** using low-tack painter's tape and securing the tape firmly. Paint the shade medium pink. Remove the tape. Allow to dry. Use the liner brush to outline each pink section with light bright green. Dip the eraser end of a pencil into violet paint to dot the white stripes of the shade.

- **Divide the lamp stem into four sections.** Paint the first section green and white checks, using a 1-inch brush.

- **Draw patterns on the lamp stem.** Paint the first section green and white checks with a 1-inch brush. Paint stripes on the second section using a 1-inch brush and violet paint; use a liner brush to add lines of bright light green, and add pink dots with a pencil eraser end. Paint the third lamp stem section the same as the surround on the armoire, using pink rosebuds and violet dimensional hearts. Base coat the fourth section pink; add vines and leaves with the liner brush and light bright green. Paint the base of the lamp light bright green; use a pencil eraser end and white paint to make dots in the green.

RIBBONS AND ROSES GIRL'S ARMOIRE

SKILL LEVEL

Intermediate

TIME

3–4 days

SUPPLIES

■ Latex paint (quart size): pure white, light pink, medium pink, light bright green, blue, violet
■ Latex brushes: 1½-inch, 3-inch
■ Artist's brushes: ½-inch flat, No. 2 small round, liner
■ Tracing paper, carbon paper
■ Pencil eraser end
■ Clear matte sealant
■ Sources on page 111

Lattice ribbon and rose patterns on page 111

RIBBONS AND ROSES GIRL'S ARMOIRE
(PROJECT SHOWN ON PAGE 46)

■ **Prime and base-coat unfinished armoire with pure white.** Paint the bottom portion of the crown molding and the beveled edges of the door panels pink. With a pencil and a ruler, lightly mark 6-inch squares on the sides of the armoire. Paint every other square pink to form a check pattern. Allow to dry.

■ **Paint the outer edges of the doors and the top of the crown molding blue.** Following the same procedure, paint them with the violet paint. Paint crown molding and door details in blue and light bright green.

■ **Size patterns** to fit your furniture piece. The lattice ribbon pattern is used for the door panels, and the roses and hearts are used on the panel surrounds. Trace the patterns onto tracing paper, and transfer the patterns onto the projects with carbon paper and a pencil. Transfer the pattern using violet paint, a ½-inch flat brush, and a small round brush. Outline the ribbons using a liner brush. Where the ribbon folds over itself, paint brush strokes to add dimension. Paint roses light pink, using a small round brush. Shade with medium pink, using a liner brush. Dot violet paint as heart-shaped accents around the roses. Paint leaves green.

■ **Seal with a coat of clear matte sealant.**

CHAIRS WITH PERSONALITY
SKILL LEVEL
Beginner
TIME
2 to 3 days
SUPPLIES
■ Paints: pale shades of yellow, blue, green, purple
■ Sealer
■ **Sources on page 111**

ADIRONDACK BENCH
SKILL LEVEL
Beginner
TIME
1 day
SUPPLIES
■ Tinted primer
■ Semigloss paint suitable for outdoor use: medium green, dark green
■ **Sources on page 111**

CHAIRS WITH PERSONALITY
(PROJECT SHOWN ON PAGE 70)
■ **This project is based on matching rockers.** Work out your color combinations before beginning the project. Sand and prime the chairs. Paint the body of each chair one color with three other colors used for accents. Seal with an exterior sealer if rocker will be used outdoors.

ADIRONDACK REVIEW BENCH
(PROJECT SHOWN ON PAGE 73)
■ **This project uses an unfinished bench** primed with tinted primer. This color scheme uses two shades of green paint suitable for exterior use. Tinted primer used under yellows, yellow-greens, and oranges provides better base color. Otherwise, these colors, which contain smaller amounts of pigment, would require additional coats of paint for coverage.

ADIRONDACK REVIEW COLOR-BLOCK CHAIRS

SKILL LEVEL

Beginner

TIME

2 days

SUPPLIES

■ Outdoor finish paint: two shades of green

■ **Sources on page 111**

ADIRONDACK REVIEW INSECT-MOTIF CHAIRS

SKILL LEVEL

Intermediate

TIME

2 days

SUPPLIES

■ Satin-finish latex paint: green, black, blue

■ Gold leaf paint

■ Wood stain: blue

■ Small artist's brush

■ Self-adhesive shelf paper

■ **Sources on page 111**

ADIRONDACK REVIEW COLOR-BLOCK CHAIRS
(PROJECT SHOWN ON PAGE 72)

■ **This project, like the Adirondack bench,** is first primed with a tinted primer. Alternate color schemes that work well for these Adirondack chairs are shades of blue or crisp white plus a primary color.

ADIRONDACK REVIEW INSECT-MOTIF CHAIRS
(PROJECT SHOWN ON PAGE 72)

■ **This project uses unfinished chairs.** Trace or sketch a simple drawing of an insect, enlarged if necessary with a photocopier. Trace the shapes onto self-adhesive shelf paper and cut out. Peel off the backs of the paper and randomly place the shapes onto the chairs. Brush on the stain lightly, carefully brushing over the paper insects and allowing the wood grain to show through. Allow to dry for 2 hours. Remove the paper, which has blocked the stain. Referring to the project photograph, hand-paint the insects with the green, blue, and black paint. Allow to dry. With small artist's brush, add gold and blue details.

GREEN FOLDING CHAIR

SKILL LEVEL

Beginner

TIME

1 day

SUPPLIES

- Polyurethane satin finish
- Flat interior latex paint: medium green, bright green, orange, golden yellow, black, white
- ½-inch artist's brush
- **Sources on page 111**

RED FOLDING CHAIR

SKILL LEVEL

Beginner

TIME

1 day

SUPPLIES

- Flat, interior latex paint: red, ochre
- ½-inch artist's brush
- Satin-finish polyurethane
- **Sources on page 111**

GREEN FOLDING CHAIR
(PROJECT SHOWN ON PAGE 71)

- **This project uses stained folding chairs.** Lightly sand the chairs, and apply one coat of stain-blocking primer. Let dry 1 hour. With a pencil, lightly draw the designs onto the seats and backs. Fill in with paint, using a ½-inch artist's brush and short, random strokes to create a mottled effect. Mix the two greens in small amounts to create color variations. Paint the sun and moon face. Let dry for 1 hour. Using a liner brush, paint the eyes and mouth of the sun and moon face. Paint the framework of the chairs black. Allow to dry. Apply three coats of polyurethane. Allow to dry completely between each coat.

RED FOLDING CHAIR
(PROJECT SHOWN ON PAGE 71)

- **Lightly sand the seat and back** of stained folding chairs. Apply one coat of stain-blocking primer. Let dry 1 hour. Paint entire chair red. Let dry 2 hours. Draw the design with white chalk and fill in with primer. Let dry 1 hour. Fill in design with ochre. Let dry 2 hours. Apply three coats of polyurethane to finish. Allow to dry completely between each coat.

DIRECTOR'S CHAIR
SKILL LEVEL
Beginner
TIME
1 day
SUPPLIES
- Flat interior latex paint: gold, pale green
- ½-inch artist's brush
- **Sources on page 111**

FRESH-AIR PORCH SWING
SKILL LEVEL
Intermediate
TIME
2 days
SUPPLIES
- Rust-preventing spray paint: white
- Oil-based stain: walnut
- Acorn finials made for fence posts
- Victorian scroll
- Drapery finials
- Wood screws
- Construction adhesive
- **Sources on page 111**

DIRECTOR'S CHAIR
(PROJECT SHOWN ON PAGE 71)
- **This project uses a director's chair with dark fabric seat and back.** Remove the fabric from the chair, and lay it out on a table covered with a drop cloth. Lightly sketch the design onto the fabric with white chalk. Fill in with two coats of gold and green paint.

FRESH-AIR PORCH SWING
(PROJECT SHOWN ON PAGE 69)
- **This project is based on a 5-foot unfinished porch swing.** Assemble the swing and attach the large finials to the bottom. Predrill holes for wood screws at the top of the back of the swing. Attach the Victorian scrolls with wood screws and construction adhesive. Attach drapery finials to the outer edges of the horizontal slat across the top, aligning them with the finials at the bottom. Brush stain over the entire swing. Allow to dry.
- **Spray with the white paint.** When the paint is dry, sand the areas that would normally show some wear so that some of the brown stain is visible.

**FRESH-AIR
WICKER CHAIR
SKILL LEVEL**
Beginner
TIME
2 days
SUPPLIES
■ Liquid deglosser
■ Acrylic spray paint:
dark green
■ Walnut stain
■ **Sources on page 111**

**FRESH-AIR END
TABLE
SKILL LEVEL**
Beginner
TIME
½ day
SUPPLIES
■ Satin-finish spray
paint: white
■ Walnut stain
■ Oil-based faux
finishing glaze
■ Embossed wallpaper
■ Wallpaper paste
■ **Sources on page 111**

FRESH-AIR WICKER CHAIR
(PROJECT SHOWN ON PAGE **69**)

■ **This project is based on a painted wicker chair.**
Do this messy project outdoors, using drop cloths
to protect the grass or patio. Clean and degloss
the chair with deglosser so paint will adhere.
Allow to dry.

■ **Spray with green paint** and allow to dry for at
least 1 hour. Brush stain over the painted finish.
To get stain into the weave of the wicker, brush
on liberally. Use a hair dryer set on cool to blow
into the crevices. Wipe the stain off the high
surfaces with a sponge. Brush out drips with a
paintbrush.

FRESH-AIR END TABLE
(PROJECT SHOWN ON PAGE **69**)

■ **Measure the top of the table** and cut the
wallpaper to fit. Glue paper to the top. Allow to
dry. Spray the piece white. Allow to dry. Wipe
with a stain mixed with glaze to enhance
detailing and embossing.

FRESH-AIR COFFEE TABLE
(PROJECT SHOWN ON PAGES **68–69**)

■ **Cut paisley shapes from the self-adhesive shelf paper.** Use the shelf paper as a stencil and place it over the bench. Lay lace over the stencil opening and spray green paint through it.

FRESH-AIR DINING TABLE
(PROJECT SHOWN ON PAGES **68–69**)

■ **Spray the base with primer and allow to dry.** Spray with the green paint. Sand areas that would normally show wear to reveal the primer beneath. This technique also works well for old stained pieces. If the base was sealed, it should be cleaned with steel wool dipped in solvent or liquid deglosser. Or use sandpaper to roughen the surface enough to hold the next coat of paint.

**FRESH-AIR
COFFEE TABLE
SKILL LEVEL**

Beginner

TIME

½ day

SUPPLIES

■ Rust-preventing spray enamel paint: medium green
■ Clear self-adhesive shelf paper
■ Large-patterned lace
■ **Sources on page 111**

**FRESH-AIR
DINING TABLE
SKILL LEVEL**

Beginner

TIME

½ day

SUPPLIES

■ Rust-preventing spray metal primer: 4 cans
■ Rust-preventing spray paint: 4 cans of medium green
■ **Sources on page 111**

PORCH WITH PUNCH BENCH

SKILL LEVEL

Intermediate

TIME

3-4 days

SUPPLIES

- Latex enamel paint: black, violet, olive green, yellow
- Acrylic paints: dark yellow, burnt umber, dark green, brick red, red
- Brushes: ½-inch flat artist's, small round, liner
- Matte spray sealant
- **Sources on page 111**

PORCH WITH PUNCH CHAIRS

SKILL LEVEL

Beginner

TIME

1 day

SUPPLIES

- Latex stain: dark gray, bright green, bright blue
- Matte latex sealant
- **Sources and pattern on page 111.**

PORCH WITH PUNCH BENCH
(PROJECT SHOWN ON PAGES 66–67)

- **Prime if the bench is unfinished.** Base-coat the following areas using a 2-inch brush: panels, yellow; panel insets and upper stiles, violet; back and lower stiles, olive green; and arms, seat, feet, and apron panels of the bottom section, black. After base-coating these areas and allowing them to dry, use a commercial stencil to add a cherry pattern or other motifs on the yellow panels.
- **Paint the stems** with the liner brush and burnt umber. Paint the leaves with a mix of dark yellow and dark green, using the ½-inch flat brush. Don't completely mix the two colors together, but leave some of the leaves with yellow areas and others with darker green areas. Paint the cherries, first with the dark yellow, then add red or brick red. Allow some of the yellow to peek through— especially in the center as a highlight. Add veins to the leaves and connect the cherries to the branches with burnt umber.
- **Make the seat pattern** marking off 3-inch sections across the front and back of the bench seat and using a straightedge to form diamonds. Mask diamond shapes and paint them olive green. Allow to dry and spray with 2 coats of matte sealant.

PORCH WITH PUNCH CHAIRS
(PROJECT SHOWN ON PAGE 66)

- **Sand the chairs with sandpaper** and wipe with tack cloth. Tape off the sections to be stained bright green. Apply the stain with a 1-inch brush and allow it to penetrate the wood. Wipe with a clean cloth. Remove tape. Tape off sections to stain blue. Apply as with the green stain. Repeat the process, using the dark gray stain. Allow to dry. Seal with 2 coats of matte latex sealant.

DINO STENCIL PATTERN PROJECT, PAGE 98

ROSE AND
HEART STENCIL
PATTERN
PROJECT,
PAGE 103

RIBBON LATTICE STENCIL PATTERN PROJECT, PAGE 103

SOURCES

Prints & Penguins: Valspar: New Green 259A-4, 236-4
Fun in California dining chairs: Minwax stains: Cherry Blossom, Mustard, Northern Ivy, Green Bayou. Behr Decorative matte finish top coat
Transferware Armoire: Valspar American Traditions exterior satin latex paint: Georgian Dark Leather 753-1. Valspar American Traditions latex paint: Amber Gold 712-1
Dining Table & Chairs: Sherwin Williams eggshell finish paint: Raffia Basket
Crackled Cupboard: Valspar paint: Weathered Oak 724-3, Ivory Hue 261-1
French Blue & White Kitchen Table: Benjamin Moore Satin Impervo paint: Blue Jean, White Dove 235 1B, California Blue 2060 20. Benjamin Moore clear matte finish sealant spray
French Chairs: Benjamin Moore Satin Impervo low-lustre enamel: Patriot Blue 2064-20, Old Blue Eyes 2064-30, Blueberry 2063-30, California Blue 2070-20, White Dove 235-1B
Burled and Aged: Valspar Decorative Effects: San Juan Hill 325-2. Valspar translucent color glaze: Burnt Sienna 95961, Mocha 96057
Aged Patina Table: Benjamin Moore interior latex eggshell finish: Linen White. Valspar Decorative Effects Crackle glaze: Porcelain 97260. Valspar Decorative Effects Antiquing glaze: Asphaltum 98278
Harlequin Armoire: Sherwin Williams Illusions Faux Finish Glazing: Navajo White, Theatre Red
Artistic Armoire: Minwax Oil-based stain: Walnut. Sherwin Williams semi-gloss enamel: Theater Red, Navajo White, Illusions Faux Finish glazing liquid.
Fun and Funky Round Cafe Table: Minwax polyacrylic satin polyurethane. Benjamin Moore flat interior latex paint: Twilight Blue 2067-30, Salsa 2009-20, Citrus Blast 2018-30, Sunshine 2021-33, Black 2132-10, White
French Blue and White Sideboard Chest: Benjamin Moore flat interior latex paint: Blue Lapis 2067-40, Super White. Briwax furniture wax, dark brown
Moroccan Table: Zinsser Bullseye Primer. Benjamin Moore Aqua Velvet: HC-7 amber, 1308 red. Minwax satin finish polyurethane

Sunflower Table: Minwax polyacrylic satin finish. Benjamin Moore flat interior latex paint: Salsa 2009-20, Yolk 2023-10, Douglas Fir 2028-20, Crushed Berries 2076-30, Peppermint Leaf 2033-20
Pale Sophisticates: Sherwin Williams flat latex paint: Dover White
White Bedroom: Behr Sugar Bowl 3B5-1
Folk Art Tray Table: Valspar Decorative Effects paint: Georgian Olive 791-3. Valspar Metal & Patina Glaze: Bronze 00178. Valspar Decorative Effects Antiquing Glaze: Asphaltum 98278
Folk Art Monogram Headboard: Valspar Decorative Effects paint: Georgian Olive 791-3. Valspar Metal & Patina Glaze: Bronze 00178. Valspar Decorative Effects Antiquing Glaze: Asphaltum 98278
Old-Fashioned Girl's Room: Laura Ashley Paints: (walls Cassiopeia 1313), 1102 Emerald 2, Chalk Pink 1, 902 Pale Cowslip 2, White
Raves for Rickrack: Sherwin Williams interior latex paint: Icy Lemonade 1667, Lovely Lilac 1829, April Green 1709, Serendipity 1708, Borage 1831, Venetian Yellow 1666.
Around the World Dresser: Sherwin Williams flat exterior latex: Red 2307. Valspar Duramax latex satin finish. Dreft One-Step Stain and Sealer: Walnut
Around the World Toy Storage Unit: Sherwin Williams oil-based semi-gloss paint: Black 6403-25692.
Around the World Tower Cabinet: Sherwin Williams semi-gloss latex paint: 1374, 1376, Red 2307, Black, Wild Iris, Yellow
Primary Colors Nursery: Krylon primer. Krylon Kids Tuff spray paint: Red, White, Yellow, Blue
Pattern-on-Pattern Girl's Room: Plaid Apple Barrel acrylics: Old Ivy, Sage Green, Canary Yellow, Wild Iris. FolkArt: Buttercrunch, Burnt Umber. Americana Deco Art: Baby Blue, Raspberry Sherbet, Glorious Gold
Dino and More: Laura Ashley paint for walls and furniture: White, Apple 3, Apple 5, Red Cayenne, Navy 4, Lilac 4, Imperial Yellow, Pumpkin 5
Sea and Sun Chest of Drawers: Minwax Polyacrylic satin finish. Benjamin Moore flat interior latex paint: Salsa 2009-20, Sunporch 2023-30, Sparkling Sun 2020-30, Snow Cone Green 2026-

30, Blue Wave 2065-50
Parisian Sketchbook Bedroom: Binz primer with sealer. Sherwin Williams latex: flat white. Pittsburgh latex satin finish: 210-4 Woodland Fern. Crayola latex satin finish: Cinderella, Lazy Days, Lilac
Cowboy Heaven Western Room Dresser: Sherwin Williams latex flat or satin paint: Black Tie 1007, Off-White 1095. Decoupage Armoire: ModPodge decoupage medium
Picture Pretty Girl's Armoire: Sherwin Williams latex enamel: Pure White, Petit Four 1297, Pink Parasol 1295, Lime Zest 1436, Violet. Dimensions: 1526, Vocal Violet 1530. Rainbow Rockers: Behr Paints: Hummingbird 1A48–4, Pineapple Souffle 1A1–3, Pixy 1A56–3, Blue Moon 1A36–3
Adirondack Bench: Valspar American Traditions semi-gloss paint: Pine Mountain 727-2, Savanna Green 861B-3
Adirondack Color Block Chairs: Valspar Color Spectrum MainPalette: Shamrock Isle 256-6, Palm Island 289
Adirondack Insect Motif Chairs: Sherwin Williams latex satin finish paint: Parrot Green, Black Tie
Terrace Green Folding Chair: Minwax polyacrylic satin finish. Benjamin Moore flat interior latex paint: Sweet Pea 2031-30, Green with Envy 2036-30, Orange Blossom 2168-30, Stuart Gold HC-10, Black 2132-10, White
Terrace Red Folding Chair: Minwax polyacrylic satin finish. Benjamin Moore flat interior latex paint: Fireball red 2170-10, Ochre 2151-30
Terrace Director Chair: Benjamin Moore flat interior latex paint: Stuart Gold HC-10, Sweet Pea 2031-30
Fresh Air Screened Porch Swing: Minwax Stain: Walnut. Rustoleum Stain Finish Spray: White.
Fresh Air Wicker Chair: Carver Trip Liquid Deglosser. Krylon satin spray paint finish: Hunter Green. Minwax stain: Walnut
Fresh Air Coffee Table: Rustoleum American Accents spray enamel: Moss Green
Fresh Air Dining Table: Rustoleum Rusty Metal Primer. Rustoleum American Accents: Moss Green
Porch with Punch Bench: Sherwin Williams enamel: Mariposa 1701, Black Tie 1007, Olive Drab 1166

CONTRIBUTORS/RESOURCES

Pages 8-9, 20-21, 29, 32, 43: Donna Talley Wendt, regional contributor; Swedish-style daybed, Blue Moon Antiques, Saratoga Springs, NY; Tria Giovan, photography
Pages 10-14: Andrea Caughey, regional editor; Erin Lyons, Mad Dog Antiques, La Jolla, CA; Ed Gohlich, photography
Pages 18-19, 23, 25, 40-41, 48-51, 58-59, 60-61, 70, 72-73: Pete Krumhardt, photography
Pages 18-19, 23, 25, 40-41, 60-61, 72-73: Wade Scherrer and Brenda Dunbar
Pages 22, 27, 44-45, 56-57, 68-69: Deborah Hastings, regional contributor; Randolph Foulds, photography
Page 24: Linda Krinn, regional contributor; Beekeeper's Cottage, Anne Carrington and Nancy Hilliard, Leesburg, VA, 703/771-9006; Ross Chapple, photography
Pages 26, 38-39, 72: Susan Andrews, regional editor; Tina Blanck, project designer, Kansas City, MO 816/333-151; Bob Greenspan, photography
Pages 28, 34-35, 71: Emily Minton, photography
Pages 28, 24, 71: Brian Carter, Atlanta, GA
Page 35: Greg Little, Studio Remontant Inc., Fort Lauderdale, FL
Pages 16-17, 42-43: Hopkins Associates,
photography
Pages 46-47, 70: Wade Scherrer
Pages 46-47, 54-55, 66-67: Joetta Moulden, regional editor; Amy Queen, project designer, Missouri City, TX, 281/321-7333; Fran Brennan, photography
Pages 48-51, 58-59, 70: Patricia Mohr Kramer
Page 19, 60-61: Wiggle Stix, (dining chairs, crib) 402 N. Main Stillwater, MN 55082 800-392-2652
Page 88: Mary Baskin, regional editor; Christi Proctor, Spice Furniture & Design, Waco, TX; Jenifer Jordan, photography

SPECIAL THANKS
Pages 18, 20, 23, 29, 51, 58, 61: Whittier Wood Products, (unfinished furniture) P.O. Box 2827, Eugene, OR 97402, 800/653-3336
Pages 72-73: Tidewater Workshop, (green chairs and bench) 800/666-8433, www.tidewaterworkshop.com
Pages 60-61: Krylon Paint, 800/797-3332; www.krylon.com
Pages: 20-21, 29, 32, 43: Benjamin Moore Paint, 800/826-2623
Pages 40-41, 58: Garnet Hill (bed linens), 800/622-6216
Pages 46-47: Swedish Style dining table, **Swedish Blonde,** 800/274-9096. Plate rack, **Lexington Home Brands,** 800/539-4636
Pages 50-51: Stamps: Rubber Stampede 72105, Little Suzy's Zoo 71014; headboard, **Woodfield's,** Clive, IA 515/727-7977
Page 57: Japanese character painting, **Itsuko McKinney,** Birmingham, AL, 205/592-3669
Pages 54-55: Club chair, ranch poster, cowhide footstool, throw pillows, lamp, wooden saddle: **Hacienda Means Home,** Houston, TX, 713/807-7150. Cowboy rug: **The Great Rug Company,** Houston, TX, 713/789-3666. Wood armoire: **Sunnyroad,** Houston, TX
Pages 46-47: Roses and Pearls pink oval rug # 1249: **The Great Rug Company.** Upholstered chair: **Sunnyroad.** Heart and teacup pottery plates and hearts: **Blue Domino,** Houston, TX Custom fabrication: **Sharon Cobetto,** Billings, MT, 406/656-5747
Pages 8-9, 32: Calico Corners, Albany, NY, 518/438-7496
Page 69: Fresh Air screened porch swing #49925: **Palmetto Mtg.,** Orangeburg, SC
Lovell & Whyte, Lakeside, MI, 616/469-5900, **The Plum Tree,** Union Pier, MI, 616/469-5980

U.S. UNITS TO METRIC EQUIVALENTS

To Convert From	Multiply By	To Get
Inches	25.4	Millimeters (mm)
Inches	2.54	Centimeters (cm)
Feet	30.48	Centimeters (cm)
Feet	0.3048	Meters (m)

METRIC UNITS TO U.S. EQUIVALENTS

To Convert From	Multiply By	To Get
Millimeters	0.0394	Inches
Centimeters	0.3937	Inches
Centimeters	0.0328	Feet
Meters	3.2808	Feet